KIN

Please renew or return items by the date shown on your receipt

www.hertsdirect.org/libraries

Renewals and enquiries: 0300 123 4049

Textphone for hearing or speech impaired 0300 123 4041

The CAMPING COOKBOOK
by ANNIE BELL

PHOTOGRAPHY BY JONATHAN BELL

Kyle Books

This edition first published in Great Britain in 2014
by Kyle Books, an imprint of Kyle Cathie Ltd.
192–198 Vauxhall Bridge Road
London, SW1V 1DX
general.enquiries@kylebooks.com
www.kylebooks.com

First Published in Great Britain in 2010 by Kyle
Cathie Ltd.

ISBN 978 0 85783 257 3

A Cataloguing in Publication record for this title is
available from the British Library.

10 9 8 7 6 5 4 3 2 1

Design: Georgia Vaux
Photography: Jonathan Bell
Editor: Vicky Orchard
Copy editor: Annie Lee
Food and props stylist: Annie Bell
Production: Gemma John

Extract on page 84 from *Swallows and Amazons* by
Arthur Ransome, published by Jonathan Cape. Reprinted
by permission of The Random House Group Ltd.
Extract on pages 72–3 from *Five Go Off in a Caravan*
(1946) by Enid Blyton © Chorion Rights Limited, a
Chorion Company. All rights reserved.

Colour reproduction by Sang Choy in Singapore
Printed and bound by Toppan Leefung Printing Ltd.
in China

CONTENTS

WHY CAMP AT ALL?

To anyone studying human behaviour from afar, it must seem puzzling that people should choose to abandon the comfort of their own home to sleep under canvas (or in a camper van, boat or caravan), which might fairly be seen as trading down. So why do we do it, and in the name of holiday at that?

We can come at this answer from any number of directions, given the tribal element of camping. One of the ironies is that while a camping trip may be fanned by a desire to escape, you only regroup once you have arrived. If you cannot define yourself in terms of 'wild camper', 'glamper', 'hiker' or 'sail camper', to mention just a handful of minorities, you still have the opportunity to join any number of camping associations that will ensure you are surrounded by like-minded people at the other end. So I can but offer a small glimpse into my own incentives or reasons why I find the notion attractive, although I am sure they will be shared by many, whatever niche compartment of the genre you belong to.

Socially, camping was popularised in the early twentieth century, and increases in popularity year on year. So much so that I cannot help but link it to the rise in our sophisticated electronic lives, which veer ever further from the basic pleasures of nature. Camping is a way of reconnecting, of stepping back from the constant onslaught of screens and technology and taking a long deep breath. The place it occupies or offers to occupy becomes ever more poignant.

When I started writing this book, one of the great surprises was discovering how many of my close friends go camping, not necessarily for weeks at a time, but for a night here and there. It has become a recreational weekend activity for many, not least because it is so accessible. Having kitted up for the first time, it is a case of keeping an eye on the weather forecast, dreaming of an adventure in some not-too-distant place, and setting off in whatever direction you choose, depending on whether you are seeking sea, mountains or rolling fields.

Talking to a neighbour the other day, he recounted the first time he took his son camping. They pitched a tent in a wood, got up in the middle of the night and set off with a pair of night-vision binoculars to watch owls. His son was instantly hooked, and the many camping trips that ensued remain precious memories of their time together. It catapulted me back to my own first experience, not so very far from home, when my brothers and I would pitch a tent in the garden and sleep there. I don't recall ever lasting much beyond five o'clock in the morning before the lure of the warmth inside the patio doors proved too great to resist, but it was long enough to experience half of the day normally denied us tucked up in our beds. The way the air cools as soon as the sun dips, seeing a moon rise and the stars come to life, even the damp air of the very early morning that cuts through to your joints as you get older, can be a pleasure.

Camping doesn't have to be far from home; despite the slightly competitive edge, you don't have to shin up a mountain and throw your pop-up tent into a slate-lined crater where no man has ever camped before in order to qualify. It's not about brownie points, there is just as much pleasure to be had from pitching a tent in a neighbouring farmer's field or a local wood and living wild for a night over the weekend as from making a huge trip. And if you have a large garden, there is plenty of fun to be had from building a camp out of sight of the house and cooking and sleeping there. Nor does it have to involve physical deprivation – should you feel you have to have a bath at night before turning in, it isn't going to lessen the experience.

But this brings me full circle to the main reason I'm into camping at all, which, at the risk of creating yet another tribe, is dinner. One of the aspects I most appreciate is the opportunity camping provides to reconnect with food in a way that reflects the surroundings. The way we cook and eat in our everyday lives has become every bit as sophisticated as our electronic existence. Food has become hugely complicated – if you buy a ready-prepared meal, be it pizza, pasta, a chicken curry or a cake, just count the number of ingredients it contains. And equally, when we are cooking at home, the style and fashion has become heavily influenced by restaurant culture, and has to compete with that glamour. To cook and serve the kind of food you might have at home on a relaxed weekend would seem out of place on a camping trip, but equally, the wonderfully simple and rustic fare that is so good eaten out of doors might seem lacking at a dinner party.

Rarely do we get the opportunity to touch base with such simple food, true to the ingredients and stripped of all unnecessary frills and steps in preparation, and that is what leads the chapters that follow. The honesty of the experience – the economy of means doesn't allow for anything else – is something to be cherished. That and its recipient counterpart, appetite, which, removed from its urban routine, acquires a new lease of life in the big outdoors. Surely together these two elements are worth all the discomfort in the world.

DAMASCENE CONVERSION

It all began with my husband's birthday, the size of which should really have left us thinking about giving up rather than embarking on camping. But trawling through the possible ways of celebrating, we settled on a boat trip along a stretch of the Thames that held happy memories for us both, with a picnic somewhere along the way. In the throes of searching for a 'vessel to hire', however, Jonnie accidentally (or so he says) clicked on the 'boats for sale' icon on a marina's website, and within the time it took to say Captain Bell, we were the proud owners of a sailing boat called *Winkle*.

It had a cabin, mind you, and that afforded us membership of the great fraternity of travellers who cook for pleasure in no fixed address, without any walls to speak of, let alone such conveniences as running water, who are known as campers. Albeit we had yet to become fully paid-up members, as hardcore campers are inclined to look on those with boats and camper vans as 'off-peak members', arguably that little bit better off than those who sleep in a tent. But full enrolment was to come.

Winkle, as you might gather from her name, is on the small side. In fact she is to yachts what micro pigs are to Gloucester Old Spots, and it took all of one very uncomfortable night and a marital tiff to realise that you would have to be a) Very Small, and b) Very Young to actually sleep on her. We were neither.

Unlike house particulars, which can be stretched, when boats/tents/ caravans advertise 'sleeps two', what they really mean is 'sleeps one-and-a-half'. Together with our son we were three. Also, with boats, unlike homes, there is no way of going up and no way of going down. All the planning permission in the world wasn't going to solve this one.

So the next logical step was a tent, which did make us fully paid-up members of the camping fraternity. I was particularly excited to discover that we even belonged to a rare tribe called 'sail campers', who travel from one destination to another by boat and camp when they get there. I suspect this coinage is actually geared towards more adventurous types who go white-water rafting along the Amazon rather than pottering up and down some half-mile of the Thames in between two locks, but we were happy all the same, and began to feel that we belonged.

As the summer unravelled and we regaled our friends and family with our new itinerant weekend status, we were amazed at how many seemed to be enjoying the occasional camping trip too. Another side to life opened up as we found ourselves planning get-togethers in unlikely places — scope for adventures new seemed endless.

Though it wasn't the easiest of learning curves. The first being that there was almost always a cavernous gap between the trip you thought you were going on and the one that actually took place. As one friend of mine put it, 'Just go assuming that you are going to have an awful time and then you'll be pleasantly surprised.' The first few trips were little short of disaster, and I am sure there will be many more of those to come. But I have learnt to pack my Zen realisation kit, and to expect the unexpected. It is an essential frame of mind, and never more so than when you are cooking dinner.

The simplicity of cooking over an open fire out of doors, with the most basic set of utensils, touches an atavistic nerve, one that is always there waiting for the chance to be rekindled. A day spent gathering together ingredients, which only ever promises surprises, whether picking in the wild or scouring unfamiliar local markets, followed by an evening round the fire or barbecue, watching the light fade and taking in the scent of food grilling and simmering as the air starts to acquire its night-time chill, is pure magic. So there you have it, a Damascene conversion. And if it can happen to me, it can happen to anyone.

GUIDE TO A GUIDE

As a cookery writer I can perhaps be forgiven for thinking that the most important aspect of camping is eating. Cooking out of doors, and the challenges it brings, are among the most enjoyable aspects of any trip. We do, however, need to begin by throwing away the rule book, and that of course creates the requisite need for a new one. Gone are the convenience of running water, upon which so much of our cooking at home depends, the shelter of walls, the oven and food processor controlled by the touch of a button. In their place comes unpredictability, and the need to cook with our wits. And that is the fun, connecting with ingredients in a fashion that is missing in our everyday lives. But with the right kit and the right approach, we have meals that will settle in our memory for years to come as some of the best we have ever eaten.

The great challenge when camping for the first time is kitting up for the occasion. Somehow, we have to try to condense the essentials of our home kitchen into a fraction of the space. There is plenty that we can live without, and the trick is to pare it down to the very minimum. There are some brilliant ergonomic designs geared towards campers, although not everything I recommend is to be found in outward-bound stores (see pages 12–24) – a great deal is just well-designed everyday equipment. The growing pressure on space in our own homes makes a lot of domestic equipment just as practical and apt on a camping trip.

When we cook at home we have a choice between hob and oven, so replicating these heat sources is the first consideration. If you are travelling very light, hiking for instance, your needs will be met by a stormproof stove such as a Trangia, the design of which holds me in awe. The entire kit unravels like a Russian doll and takes up the space of a medium-sized saucepan. Within it you have your heat source, a couple of saucepans, a frying pan and a kettle. However, if weight and space are less of an issue you may want to run to a camping gas stove. But for most people the addition of a travelling barbecue will open the way to evenings spent relaxing in the open, drawing in the scent of food on the grill. It may not always be possible to rustle up an open fire, although when it is you have the option of cooking on a tripod, or grilling over the fire. So all the recipes here are geared for one of these two cooking mediums, single ring or barbecue, each of which is signalled by an icon beside the method.

Having packed up your kitchen, the next consideration is how to squeeze the contents of your storecupboard into the small space that remains. If we have to take just one little part of the world with us on our trip, then let that be the Mediterranean. The scents and flavours of its shores capture everything that is alluring about cooking out of doors. The Travelling Storecupboard that follows is the Mediterranean in your pocket.

Bringing it all together are the essentials of olive oil, lemon juice and garlic. So step number one is to combine these ingredients in convenience form before you leave: this is the Camping Marinade (see page 27), a golden key. On its own you need nothing further for meat and fish destined for the grill, but with the addition of a few succinct spice blends you broaden your horizons. These spices can either be prepared at home before you go, or you can order them online (see pages 28–9). A second key, albeit smaller, is Camping Glaze (see page 28), a blend of honey and mustard, which you can use to coat meat and fish and also combine with the Camping Marinade to create a delicious salad dressing.

From here the recipe chapters take you from dawn until dusk, starting with hearty Cowboy Brunch to banish the morning chill and set you up for the day's recreation ahead, and taking you right through to the other end of the day with recipes for making a comforting mug of cocoa with a drop of rum and biscuits to dunk, before you retire to your sleeping bag. In between, children can be packed off on a 'Famous Five' adventure with a full-on picnic tea; there is a chapter on speedy appetisers and little eats, should you make new friends or have old ones visiting; and the supper-time chapters revolve around one-pot dishes, with lots of recommendations for travelling barbecues, including more ambitious dishes like butterflied shoulder of lamb and a whole salmon steamed between long wild grasses. There is also a chapter on cakes to make and take with you, some of which can be used to create puddings. And of course, there are all the camping favourites like bananas baked in their skins and toasted marshmallows.

At the heart of all of this is the essential consideration: a lack of water. All the recipes are designed to keep your need for it to a minimum, not only in the preparation of food but also in the washing up. A stack of greasy saucepans, a plastic washing-up bowl and cold water can very quickly erase the magic of the meal that's just been eaten, so I promise that at the very most you might have one pan to clean. Nor do the recipes involve scales, an unnecessary item to lug along, which makes for the wrong mindset generally. Instead measurements are a relaxed 'handful', 'tablespoon', 'tin mug', and the like.

Writing this in the middle of winter, I can't wait for next summer to go camping again, and start planning the next feast. Although I may not wait until the holidays come round, and you just might find me of a weekend in my field kitchen at the bottom of the garden, playing camping. It's hard to resist.

ESSENTIAL KIT

Before kitting up to camp for the first time, I glanced around my kitchen – all those treasured items. And suddenly that old adage 'everything but the kitchen sink' acquired meaning.

The question begging here is when does 'essential' become 'non essential'? It will have everything to do with how you normally cook at home and how much you feel you are able to sacrifice, a choice that is euphemistically known as 'subjective'. A good peppermill, for instance, is non-negotiable in my book. Camping shops may sell those little push-button mills, brilliant in design but soulless in action. The satisfying sensation and scent of black peppercorns grinding at a twist of the wrist, and the scrunch of a flaky sea salt between my fingers, are rituals I cannot imagine foregoing before putting food on to the grill or into the pot.

Equally you may have some large, unwieldy, heavy pot that cooks in a particular way and gives you a huge amount of pleasure to use out of doors. So pack it up and squeeze it in. Unless you're hiking, in which case your choice of kit will be necessarily austere, there is every chance you will be travelling by car, and just might be able to make room. Much of what follows isn't available from camping stores or even designed with campers in mind, it's just well designed and ergonomic.

I reckon I can fit the whole caboodle into a reasonable-sized wooden box (which doubles as a prep table once unpacked), with a separate small box by way of a 'travelling storecupboard', a barbecue and stove, and a couple of cold bags. Each recipe that follows lists below it the basics of what will be required to cook it, without listing the obvious like a chopping board, utensils and plates to eat from.

Cooking

BARBECUE

There are some brilliant designs of portable barbecue out there, and they seem to get more compact by the year. But there is a big difference between being ergonomic and cooking like a dream. And just because they fold away to next to nothing doesn't mean they necessarily perform well.

If you are used to cooking on a kettle barbecue it is difficult to conceive of going back to an open one, where the heat is difficult to control and the wind whips up the ash and fans the flames. There are various options here, but Weber's iconic charcoal kettle, designed by George Stephen in 1951 in Chicago, remains a brilliant piece of design. Later it became known as the Sputnik after its resemblance to the Russian satellite.

Stephen fashioned his prototype from a shipping buoy, by cutting it in half, sticking legs in the base, cutting vents top and bottom to control the heat, and using the top as a lid. All kettle barbecues today are based on this principle. The lid not only reduces flare-ups but creates an oven so that the food cooks inside at the same time as charring on the outside. It also serves to keep out the rain and wind, making it the best possible all-weather option.

Travel kettle barbecue

The 'Smokey Joe Gold', a miniature kettle barbecue, is a little bulkier than other portable types, but if you have the space it's a guarantee of great results. The handle clips over the lid so you can carry it without any ash falling out, or even move it from place to place once it's lit. You can also employ the indirect method, in which the coals are piled up on either side, for cooking slightly larger cuts and meat and fish on the bone that take longer than 20 minutes, which is about the limit for grilling over a fierce heat without burning.

Weber's 'Go-Anywhere', which is shaped like a box, works on the same system, and opens out into a grill. www.weber.com

Cobb Barbecue

The Cobb is an ingenious travelling barbecue. First dreamt up in the townships of South Africa as a green and fuel-efficient way of cooking, it was originally fuelled by corn cobs, hence its name. It finds more and more fans every year. The great pluses are the travelling case, which means you can pack it up and go while it is still hot; the speed with which it heats up if you use a cobblestone rather than briquettes, and that it can roast a whole chicken and potatoes (a meal which, for many of us, is a holy grail whether camping or at home), in addition to smaller cuts.

It's a great system if you're away for a night or a weekend and have access to a dishwasher at the end. The bowl contains a moat that collects the fat from the food as it grills, which isn't something you want to be tackling with a plastic bowl in the middle of nowhere. So for hardcore campers with limited facilities I'd recommend a traditional barbecue such as a small Weber, in which the fat burns off the grill as the food cooks and it can be cleaned with a wire brush or piece of crumpled foil at the end – no water required. The cobblestones are available by mail order from their website (www.cobb-bbq.co.uk) and from Lakeland (see Stockists, p172).

Chimney starter

Not essential but a piece of kit that makes lighting a barbecue exceptionally easy – a hollow metal tube with holes around the outside, which is filled with charcoal and lit with newspaper from below. Within 30–40 minutes the charcoal is furnace-hot. www.weber.com

Wire brush

There's no scrubbing of pots and pans with a barbecue, just a quick rub down for the grill once it's cooled down. The ideal is a wire brush, although scrumpled foil can be used in its absence.

STOVE

Trangia is the original stormproof expedition stove, first produced in the 1920s, and today it is regulation issue for the Swedish military. It opens out like a Russian doll, the size of a cake tin, and it contains two small saucepans and a frying pan that doubles as a lid, a kettle and a burner.

Most other camping stoves of the same ilk are copies of this one. More recently they have introduced anodised ultra-light aluminium versions that provide a non-stick surface. These come with the option of fuel or gas. www.amazon.co.uk

Alternatively, the slightly bulkier option is a gas stove. The larger of these will have two rings, and it's worth buying one with a windshield. For a family of four away for a week who are likely to be cooking a fair deal this is likely to be more practical. www.milletts.co.uk

Gas or fuel

Given the many challenges of cooking out of doors, it is a complete joy to be able to command heat for your food at the touch of a button. The most portable single-ring systems such as the Trangia will have a small gas attachment, while the larger camping gas stoves will come with a bottle. You get a longer burn time with gas than you would with spirit or meths, so if you have slow or one-pot cooking in mind, gas is a more practical option.

However, a small spirit burner such as the Trangia provides the most portable solution to a single ring, with the advantage that you have a ready supply of fuel in a comparatively small bottle. The downsides are the relatively brief cooking time (meths will do for up to 45 minutes in a Trangia), and the lack of control over the heat, which can be set either at simmer or boil but rarely in between, so for more sophisticated cooking this can be an issue. But if all you want is to boil a kettle and maybe fry some bacon in the morning, or heat up some soup, then it's all you need.

TRIPOD AND DUTCH OVEN See page 21.

Storage

COLDBOX

Even the most efficient cold boxes or bags only work to keep food at the temperature in which it is put into the box, as opposed to chilling it down in the fashion of a fridge. Every time you open up that lid, you are allowing a little warm air to get in.

Days one and two of camping are relatively easy on this front. If you chill your food down well before leaving, a good cold box should keep it at that temperature. It also works well to freeze things like sausages and barbecue meats – small cuts should have thawed by the evening, while anything larger will last overnight, acting as an ice-pack in the process. But otherwise, shopping is something to look upon as a daily activity, a pleasure when it involves seeking out a local market, farm shop or little fish shop in a seaside village.

For the purposes of travelling light, there are some brilliant material cold bags, which are the ones I favour when tootling down the Thames in our little boat – they can be squeezed into lockers, and fold down to nothing once they are empty. Lakeland's Flectalon-lined cool bags work like a thermos (Flectalon is a reflective silvered material that was originally developed for NASA astronauts in space). The food remains at the same temperature as when it is put into the bag, even when left in the sun. A couple of these allows one for food and one for drinks. www.lakeland.co.uk

THERMOS

It's worth taking a thermos of hot water – even if not for drinks, it'll come in handy for washing up. Or fill it with lovely chilled water for drinking. The Thermos Work Series Steel Flask keeps liquid either hot or cold for 24 hours. www.amazon.co.uk

JERRYCAN

The ideal is a jerrycan that will pour while lying on the ground, otherwise you need a table to place it on. Another solution is an enamel jug that you can decant into. www.outdoor-kitchen.biz

PLASTIC STORAGE CONTAINERS

Hard to imagine camping without a set of plastic storage containers. These have come a long way since the early days of Tupperware, which has been superseded by containers with wings on the lid that clip down on to the base. Lock & Lock are the original of their type and are 100 per cent airtight and spillproof. Brilliant for anything messy that needs to go into the cold box, as well as for marinating foods – you can shake them without any risk of leakage, which does away with a lot of messy mixing. A stackable set of about seven should do you for all your requirements, including the Camping Marinade and Camping Glaze. The corners of square ones are good for pouring. www.johnlewis.co.uk and www.jwpltd.co.uk

STACKABLE BOWLS

A set of colourful plastic preparation bowls travel light and will double as serving dishes. Joseph Joseph make excellent sets, the larger of which also encompass a sieve, a colander and either measuring spoons or a lemon squeezer. www.josephjoseph.com. We also love lightweight bamboo bowls, a renewable source of material and green option. www.greentulip.co.uk

TRAVELLING POTS

For the sake of a few days away we only need small quantities of essentials for the storecupboard. I find the ideal are lightweight aluminium screw-top tins (about 100ml), which are non-breakable and perfect for spice mixes, sugar, salt and the like. These are available from cosmetic suppliers, who also have small aluminium bottles that are good for decanting liquids and oils. www.naturallythinking.com

Preparation

CHOPPING BOARD

Worth every inch of space, this will double as a work surface in challenging situations where you don't have a table. A folding one makes good sense. www.josephjoseph.com.
Cork chopping boards are a good lightweight option, and they float, if that is a consideration. www.greentulip.co.uk

KNIVES
One small and one large sharp knife

Hard to get away with less. A chef's travelling canvas holdall will contain not only these but a can opener and corkscrew too. www.nisbets.co.uk

Serrated knife

Great for tomatoes and salamis, and less likely to slip than other knives if you are cooking anywhere rough. This will also double up as a travel-size bread knife for baguettes, flatbreads and small loaves.

Pocket knife

For one night away and light cooking you may be able to get away with a pocket knife without any additional ones. If it has attachments such as a bottle opener, corkscrew and scissors, so much the better.

Chopper

This bit of non-essential gadgetry is a trip back in time. I remember when my parents returned one year from their annual pilgrimage to the Ideal Homes Show, where they would always arrive back in a state of excitement with the latest toy that was going to change their lives. These choppers are still around, in better form than ever – the stainless steel version is good and sturdy and does away with the need for knives when chopping onions and the like. They're tear-free too. www.rosle.com

Other Implements

A potato peeler
Or not...you may be happy with small baked potatoes or new ones cooked in their skins. But otherwise there is only one, the REX, a staple in professional kitchens. www.nisbets.co.uk
A wooden spoon or two
A can opener
A corkscrew
A ladle if you are cooking soup or stews
Tongs

Pots and pans

If you have a camping stove such as the Trangia, you may be kitted out with a few basic pans, frying pan and kettle already. The advantage here is that they are lightweight and pack to nothing; the disadvantage is that they are more likely to burn food, and they tend to come on the small side. As an alternative to these, whatever you have in the kitchen will do. At the very least I would take a good-sized non-stick frying pan.

LARGE POT OR PAN
This is essential to one-pot dishes. If you are cooking on a sturdy Campingaz stove, there is no reason not to lug your favourite cast iron casserole with you. But my favourite large dedicated camping pot, which ticks all the boxes, is a Trangia Billy Can (such as the 4.5 litre one). Made of lightweight aluminium, it also has a handle for hanging, so you can use it for tripod cooking as well. www.amazon.co.uk. Another option if you plan on cooking on a tripod over an open fire is the Lodge system (see Dutch oven, right).

DUTCH OVEN

While hefty, these big cast iron pots really come into their own when you are either slow or one-pot cooking. If you buy one with a handle designed to hang on a tripod you'll have the wherewithal for cooking over a log fire. The American cast iron foundry Lodge has been catering to itinerant cooks since 1896. A cast iron skillet and Dutch oven were normally the only pieces of cookware early American families possessed. These pots have small feet on them, which is worth bearing in mind if you also want to use one on a gas ring, as you would need an ordinary cast iron pot for this. Lodge also produce a 'potlifter' for use on the tripod, to keep an eye on the food as it cooks.
www.eddingtons.co.uk

DREAM-POT

I was very sceptical about how useful I would find one of these Australian portable slow cookers, but it only took two or three times of using it to realise just how indispensable it might become. It could have been designed around a tiffin carrier: two saucepans – one very large and one smaller one that fits into the top – will hold two different dishes, perfect for stews or casseroles with rice, for instance. The idea is that you start cooking with these, for perhaps a quarter of the usual cooking time, and then pop them into your Dream-Pot, which has an outer casing that works like a thermos. It clips shut and has a handle for carrying it. The food continues to cook very slowly, and is perfectly cooked and piping hot 2–3 hours later. It cannot overcook, even if you leave it for 7 hours, but would simply require a little reheating at that point.

I find the Dream-Pot is brilliant for short camping trips, when perhaps you set off a few hours in advance of reaching your destination.

FRYING PAN

A good-sized non-stick frying pan is central to fry-ups. There are now some excellent 'green' non-stick frying pans on the market, such as the 'GreenPan', which has a thermalon coating. Almost like enamel, it is in fact ceramic, and we can fry away with a clear conscience that we're not harming the environment or ourselves. www.aolcookshop.co.uk

COLANDER

If you have one of the stackable sets of bowls (see page 18) you are sorted, but otherwise a plastic collapsible colander folds flat. Most of the recipes are designed to get around the need, but they're useful for washing fresh fruit and veg. www.josephjoseph.com

Eating

PLATES

Most hardware stores will have biodegradeable plates, bowls and the like. The Rolls Royce of these, however, are made from bamboo veneer. They are designated single use, but if it's just a few crumbs they can be wiped down and reused. www.greentulip.co.uk. Otherwise enamelware remains a classic and practical camping option. www.surplusandoutdoor.com

CUTLERY

Knives, forks and teaspoons can all be obtained in biodegradeable materials, which will save on the washing up. But a teaspoon and tablespoon are essential measures in the recipes that follow.

TIN MUG

An essential measurement in many of the recipes that follow, a little over 300ml in capacity. So if you decide not to take one, it's worth checking that your mugs are about the same volume.

TUMBLERS

We can live without long-stemmed glasses; they only ever fall over. One tumbler suits all.

SKEWERS

Wooden ones that can be burnt at the end of the barbecue are ideal – soak them in water first. But a few metal ones won't take up much space and can take on a little more strain. Flat ones will ensure the food doesn't slip around.

SALT AND PEPPER

Using a peppermill is second nature in the kitchen. I was dreading having to leave my Peugeot mill at home (these are widely regarded as the best grinding mechanisms), but they also produce an adorable mouse of a mill called the 'Bistro' that measures 7cm (www.chomette.co.uk). As for the crunchy salt, also *de rigueur*, an empty cigar or vanilla tube does nicely.

And don't forget

BRIQUETTES
Charcoal briquettes tend to burn more faithfully than lumpwood, which can be erratic.

FIRELIGHTERS
There are special firelighters for barbecues that don't smell of paraffin. www.weber.com

LONG MATCHES

FOIL
In the absence of an oven, foil is endlessly useful for baking food in a parcel on the barbecue, as well as for lining a frying pan, for instance when cooking bacon. 'Green' foil uses about 90 per cent less energy than standard foil.

RUBBISH BAGS
A variety of sizes comes in handy, but especially small ones.

NICETIES LIKE TENTS
For a great one-stop camping shop, with a range of 'fashion' tents for glampers, which we love, try Millets. www.millets.co.uk

When circumstances allow, there is nothing quite like sleeping under proper canvas. This company produce generously sized traditional white canvas bell tents, with or without integrated ground sheets, that make camping seem almost luxurious. www.belltent.co.uk

Camping tends to bring out the Scot in us, so here's a wide range of plastic-backed picnic rugs that fold down to nothing. www.tartanrugs.com

TRAVELLING STORECUPBOARD

A travelling storecupboard is the golden key. But how daunting, to pare all those different oils and vinegars, bottled sauces, spices and dried herbs down to a desert island collection of essentials. Or, as my husband puts it, 'How many types of peppercorn does a girl need?' Answer: seven. On the other hand, it is liberating to discover just how little you really need to create a wonderful range and array of dishes.

Life is made that much easier by homing in on just one flavour palette – and for a life outdoors that has to be the Mediterranean. The intensity of flavour, the colour, the sheer panache and relaxation that go hand in hand with the food of Spain, Italy, Greece, the Middle East and North Africa capture so much of what we are seeking when we pack up our caravans and camper vans, or load the tents and sleeping bags into the car, idly looking ahead to the moment when we will light the fire and while away the hours gazing into the flames and drawing in the scent of meat or seafood sizzling on the grill.

Bringing it all together, a luscious green olive oil, the sharp relief of fresh lemon juice, the pungency of garlic and a good sea salt. So step one in creating our 'travelling storecupboard' is to combine all these into what will be called Camping Marinade, which takes all of 5 minutes before you go.

Dressed simply with this elixir, lamb chops, chicken pieces, a steak or pork fillet will be divine with a simple green salad and some warmed flat breads in tow. And it's easy to take it one step further with the addition of a succinct spice blend. Again you don't need anything extensive here: a Moroccan and a Middle Eastern blend will have a myriad of uses.

Allowed to sneak in a couple of extras, a little sachet of Jerk Seasoning is possibly my favourite barbecue classic, and some zahtar (a blend of toasted sesame seeds, thyme and sumac) can be sprinkled over warm flatbreads drizzled with oil for the simplest of pizza-style breads, scattered over grilled chicken or simple salads of grilled vegetables, also over dressed green leaves.

Two more ingredients that I use endlessly at home are honey and Dijon mustard. These can be combined into what will be known as Camping Glaze, which can be used to give chicken, sausages and the like a lovely sticky finish on the grill. It can also be mixed with the Camping Marinade to create a fab salad dressing. A handful of basics in addition are all that you need. You may not want everything that's suggested, but whip up the basic marinade and glaze and you have the foundation for pretty much everything you might want to barbecue or serve as a salad.

Marinade and glaze

CAMPING MARINADE

Good for a couple of meals for 3–4 people

This marinade is perfect as it stands – you need go no further in dressing meat or fish for the grill. But equally you can use it as a building block, by adding herbs such as thyme, oregano or marjoram, rosemary or herbes de Provence. Or you can add one of the suggested spice blends (see page 29) to whisk you to the shores of Morocco or to the Middle East. Either way, this means you are effectively working with only two ingredients while you are cooking.

100ml lemon juice (2–3 lemons)
150ml extra virgin olive oil
3 garlic cloves, peeled and crushed to a paste
1 teaspoon sea salt

Combine all the ingredients in an airtight container, such as Lock & Lock (see page 18) and shake before use. Store in a cool place.

CAMPING GLAZE

Good for a couple of meals for 3–4 people

Possibly my all-time favourite glaze, for everything from the skin of roast chicken to chipolatas and cocktail sausages. Combine it with the elixir on the previous page and you have a delicious honey mustard salad dressing. It's easy to whip up more of this, should you require, but this is a good amount to start off with.

4 tablespoons Dijon mustard
4 tablespoons set honey

Blend the two ingredients in a bowl and store in an airtight container, such as Lock & Lock (see page 18).

Spices

If you are to take just two blends with you, it is the Middle Eastern and Moroccan blends that are used most extensively in the recipes that follow.

Although there is no need to take these, or the Jerk Seasoning or herbes de Provence, any further than blending them with olive oil and using them as a marinade or to coat whatever you are grilling, they promise tantalisingly good results, with scents that will whisk you off to foreign shores and beaches.

By far the easiest route is to order the spices online from Seasoned Pioneers (www.seasonedpioneers.co.uk), who specialise in replicating traditional spice blends. 'Annie's Camping Kit' has all five spice blends that feature in the book. These conveniently come in small lightweight resealable packets, an ideal travel size. But below are recipes too for making the key blends yourself (herbes de Provence and zahtar are best bought ready-made). You can either grind the spices yourself or use them ready-ground.

MIDDLE EASTERN SPICE BLEND (*KABSA*)

This fiery blend is scented with that Middle Eastern duo – cinnamon and cumin.

1½ teaspoons cayenne pepper
1 teaspoon cinnamon
1½ teaspoons cumin
1 teaspoon black pepper
½ teaspoon nutmeg
½ teaspoon cardamom
¼ teaspoon cloves
½ teaspoon coriander

Note: green cardamom will probably require sifting once ground.

MOROCCAN SPICE BLEND (*LA KAMA*)

Mellow, peppery and sweet – ginger, black peppercorns, turmeric, cinnamon, nutmeg.

2 teaspoons ginger
2 teaspoons black pepper
1 teaspoon turmeric
1 teaspoon cinnamon
½ teaspoon nutmeg

JERK SEASONING

This has always been a curiosity with its intriguing barbs – allspice, thyme and nutmeg – that make such a classic combination. It's worth packing this for making Jerk chicken alone, but it will be fab with any meat or fish.

3 teaspoons onion powder
2 teaspoons black pepper
2 teaspoons light muscovado sugar
1 teaspoon allspice
1 teaspoon dried thyme
1 teaspoon dried chilli flakes
½ teaspoon ground nutmeg
½ teaspoon cloves

Note: there is no need to grind the thyme or chilli flakes here.

A few basics

Extra virgin olive oil
Sea salt
Black pepper
Chilli flakes or Tabasco
Sugar
Dark rum

ALL SYSTEMS CAMPING

A minimal investment of time and preparation before you leave home will make a world of difference to the smooth running of any camp kitchen. More than anything it's about taking advantage of constant running water to get the messy little tasks like squeezing lemons and crushing garlic out of the way, hence the all important Camping Marinade, designed to be whizzed up at home before you leave.

THINGS TO DO BEFORE YOU GO

Make up Camping Marinade and Camping Glaze (see pages 27–8)
Order or make up spice blends (see pages 28–9)
Freeze ice-bags
Bake a cake (see pages 58–69)

Wash fruit, vegetables and salad leaves
Sharpen knives
Fill thermos
You could also
Make some garlic butter (see page 150)
Prepare some crushed garlic in olive oil

First build your kitchen

Although this would seem to be obvious, as a novice I found it wasn't. The first night we set off 'sail camping' in *Winkle*, I was so relieved to reach our destination, and so hungry from the journey, that I got straight into preparing dinner without considering how to make the whole thing work practically. Within no time our pitch took on refugee status. It was impossible to cook in, with the jerrycan at one end, a chopping board on the grass somewhere in the distance, and the essential kit strewn all over the place. So now I know better – that ten minutes of Girl Guide organisation makes all the difference.

The great essential is water, as you are almost certainly going to have to transport it by hand to wherever you are cooking. So first there's a need for a carrier or jerrycan, and I also like to have a big enamel jug and basin that take over from there by way of a tap and sink. Second is the need for somewhere to chop or prepare food, which is all but impossible at ground level, but equally doesn't need to be as high as a table either. Our solution is a big old wooden box that serves to carry the equipment around, and that, once unpacked, can be upturned into a table of sorts. And last, you need a bin or plastic bag. There is, of course, endless other paraphernalia to organise or stack away, but sort the basics and the rest will fall into place.

A LITTLE KNOW-HOW

Keeping cold

The slim flat ice blocks seem to give the best coverage within a cold bag or box, and can be stacked between items. But in their absence, an empty milk carton filled with water and frozen is a good make-do. Then, of course, there is the problem of what to do when they have defrosted. Some campsites will have a freezer, but otherwise, at the risk of being a little cheeky, you could always ask in a shop with an ice-cream fridge if you can pop your ice-blocks into it to cool down. Most shops with a half-empty freezer will be happy to oblige.

Stoves  = Recipes using stove

COOKING WITH METHS

There is little in the way of adverse weather conditions that a stormproof camping set will not be able to cope with. But they do call for a little know-how.

Using a meths burner, you get a burn time of around 25 minutes on high – this is when the small holes at the base are facing the wind and the air is drawn up past the burner, making it heat the food as fast as possible.

By slowing things down you can double the cooking time: either turn the holes at the base away from the wind, or pop the simmer ring on top of the burner, to extinguish the outer edge of the flame. If you do run out of meths mid-cook, remove the pan, place the burner cap over the burner (having removed the rubber ring inside) and, once the flame has gone out give it a minute or two to cool, then fill and relight it.

One further tip, to help with the washing up, is to add 10 per cent water to your meths, which will reduce the amount of carbon deposits on the pans.

COOKING WITH GAS

If anything differs from cooking with gas at home, it is trying to achieve a really low heat, which can be a little hazardous outdoors where the flame so easily blows out. I would set the flame at a minimum of medium, even when trying to cook a dish very gently.

Barbecues ⌇⌇ = Recipes using barbecue

Travelling barbecues, however fantastic, are limited by their size. At home, where we tend to have larger barbecues, we are used to being able to spread out on the grill and cook meat, fish and vegetable accompaniments all at once, whereas a travelling barbecue effectively has the capacity of a single ring. While it will do you proud grilling meat or fish for supper, if you want cooked vegetables too you need either a single burner on which to heat a pan, a second travelling barbecue, or to settle instead for a salad and flatbreads that are quickly warmed on the grill at the end.

LIGHTING UP

The ultimate foolproof way of lighting a charcoal barbecue is a chimney starter (see page 15). Coals are piled into an open-ended cylinder, while a couple of pieces of scrunched-up newspaper in the base are enough to light the briquettes. Leave it for half an hour or so, standing it on the barbecue grid, and you should have red hot coals coated in the desirable film of light grey ash that signifies they are ready for grilling. Tip them over the grid of the barbecue and off you go.

In the absence of one of these, the principle for lighting coals is pretty much the same. Build a pyramid of coals on your barbecue grid, with a firelighter on the bottom, and once they are dusted in ash, spread them out on the grid. The mistake so often made is to spread them out on the grid in the first place – you end up using half a packet of firelighters, and the coals at the extremes never catch on.

As to logs, start the fire in a small way with lots of kindling, paper and a couple of firelighters, and as it appears to be taking hold, build it up a log at a time. The ideal here is small logs rather than the kind you might put on the grate in the heart of winter.

COBB BARBECUE KNOW-HOW

With a Cobb barbecue you have a choice of two fuel mediums: on the one hand you can use a small number of briquettes, which will give you a gentle temperature, or you can use a cobblestone, which cooks at a higher temperature – this is great, a single fuel-efficient block made from coconut shells, which are a renewable energy source. It is hot within 5–10 minutes of being lit and provides 2 hours of cooking. These would be my recommendation for any of the barbecuing recipes that follow.

The grill plate effectively sears the meat, so you need to keep turning a whole chicken, for instance. But it produces beautifully tender and succulent results, with little risk of burning that can take place with other barbecues. It also allows you to bake small jacket potatoes that again might burn in a hotter barbecue.

WEBER OR KETTLE BARBECUE KNOW-HOW

Kettle barbecues cook in two ways, either by the 'direct' method, where the coals are spread out on the grid in the usual fashion, or by the 'indirect' method, where they are piled at either side, which enables you to cook a larger cut of meat on the bone without fear of it burning. The cooking times here are on a par with a hot oven at home, which makes life easy, as there is no great adjustment to make.

COWBOY BRUNCH

Being part of the morning as it comes to life, separated only by a sheet of canvas, is one of the great joys of camping – experiencing the light as it changes, the scents, and the way the damp is driven into remission by the sun, if you're lucky. I can almost forgive the unfamiliarity of a mattress that hasn't lost a single opportunity during the night to remind me that I'm not at home, blocking every attempt to turn with its hard line on comfort. So it's up at dawn, and by the time the sun has reached the treetops my appetite has kicked in with a long-forgotten lust for the first meal of the day.

The ideal is a proper, big breakfast, to lounge around drinking mugs of strong black coffee, drawing in the smell of bacon and eggs sizzling in the frying pan, which just might jolt any lazy loungers to surface and join you. And kippers gently smoked over an open fire or a Huckleberry Finn-style frying pan of crispy fish and bacon acquire an irresistible allure – fantasy breakfasts, but also not beyond reach. With a little cunning you can even land your bacon and eggs without the big greasy frying pan that normally comes in its wake. And what is that craving for toast slathered with unsalted butter and marmalade or apricot jam, something that normally I can live without from one year to the next?

So the idea here is to satisfy this long-lost friend, appetite, and tuck into breakfast in a frenzy of enthusiasm before going off and climbing a mountain or surfing a few waves, returning to base camp mid-afternoon for a cuppa tea and a piece of cake, before settling to the serious business of supper.

TOAST AND JAM

The craving? I suspect it may be a kind of perverse challenge to the elements and circumstances, because, of the simplest delights, at the outset it presents itself as insurmountable without an electric toaster. And if there is one thing likely to drive our passion then surely it is the elusive. But we WILL have toast. So pack a jar of some particularly fine homemade jam – I have a thing about apricot with unsalted butter, but greengage or plum, a chunky strawberry or a thick marmalade are all going to seem equally heavenly with that steaming cup of coffee.

SIMPLY TOAST

The quick route to satiating that craving is to heat a dry frying pan over a medium flame and toast the **bread** for a couple of minutes a side as you like it.

Kit Stove, frying pan

FLAME-GRILLED TOAST

The route here depends on the nature of the bread. Sourdough, for instance, and other country breads that are normally slow to colour in an electric toaster, fare best when drizzled with olive oil before grilling, while more delicate crumbs, such as ordinary sliced white, will be fine without oil.

The time the toast takes will depend on the heat of the grill, but on a hot barbecue you should work according to the timing you would expect at home from a toaster – maybe 1–2 minutes each side for bread with a delicate crumb, and 2–3 minutes for **sourdough** drizzled with **oil**.

Kit Barbecue

SPANISH TOAST

Living in Seville for a while, breakfast at a bar round the corner was a cup of industrially strong coffee and a thick baguette-like slab of bread, toasted, drizzled with olive oil and spread with jam. The advantage for campers, obviously, is the lack of any butter.

Simply toast your **bread** in a dry frying pan over a medium heat for a couple of minutes a side until golden. Drizzle with **oil**, or do this first if you want something really crispy, then spread with **jam**.

Kit Stove, frying pan

CHOCOLATE TOASTIES

For 2 people

Assuming you don't have access to a pâtisserie, these louche little pittas hark back to the days before *pains au chocolat* became our weekend treat, when French children would munch on a length of baguette and a stick of chocolate on their way to school.

Heat a frying pan over a medium-low heat. Slit 2 **mini pitta breads**, pop a row of **dark chocolate** squares within each, and grill for several minutes each side, until the chocolate has melted.

Kit Stove, frying pan, sharp knife

RASPBERRY PANCAKE

For 1 person

This continues to play to the need for warmth and comfort first thing, easily turned out in any number with pancakes or oatcakes, a personal favourite. I always get very excited by finding wild blueberries and such like until, at closer inspection, they turn out to be deadly poisonous – but there are plenty of blackberries to be had from August onwards, and pick-your-own and farm shops will fill in with various berries earlier in the season.

Heat a large non-stick frying pan over a medium heat. Spread a tablespoon of **raspberry jam** over half a **pancake**, scatter a handful of **raspberries** on top and close with the other half, gently pressing the fruit down. Cook for about a minute a side until warmed through.

Kit Stove, frying pan, spatula

FRENCH TOAST

For 2 people

Also known as *pain perdu* or lost bread, the art here lies in caramelising at the edges with a little honey. It's divine, whether you play to its savoury side with crispy bacon, or smother it in more honey, maple or golden syrup, or jam. It also makes a fine stand-in for a bread and butter pud with some cream at the other end of the day. You don't get away scot-free in terms of the washing up, but provided your pan is non-stick a quick wipe with a piece of kitchen paper should do it.

1 medium egg
$^1/_3$ of a tin mug of milk
1 tablespoon caster sugar
butter for frying
2 teaspoons honey
2 slices of white bread or brioche

Whisk the egg with the milk and sugar in a shallow bowl. Heat a non-stick frying pan over a medium heat, add a knob of butter and the honey, and once these are sizzling, dip the bread into the egg and milk mixture and fry either side until golden and caramelised around the edges. Spoon any gooey pan juices over. If you need to do them one at a time, use just a teaspoon of honey for each slice.

Kit Stove, frying pan, spatula

BACON SARNIES

For 2 people

To eat a warm bacon sandwich out of doors on a morning that's slowly coming to life is to restore one's faith in appetite. And here, so as not to relinquish any of the magic, there is no frying pan to wash at the end.

Line a large frying pan with foil, lay 5–6 rashers of **rindless streaky bacon** in the pan and cook over a medium heat until golden either side. You may find they don't colour as evenly as usual on their bed of foil, so keep an eye on them and move them around as necessary. Now slip the foil out of the pan, warm a **pitta bread**, slit it in half, fill with the bacon, and dollop over some **ketchup or HP sauce**.

With egg

You can fry a couple of eggs in the rendered bacon fat left on the foil, with an additional drizzle of oil to assist in basting the yolk.

Kit Stove, frying pan, foil, sharp knife, spatula for egg

KIPPERS WITH BROWN BREAD

It was one of those perfect meals (even though we weren't camping at the time) – a windy Hebridean beach with a canopy of blue sky, a fire made with driftwood on the edge of the dunes, and kippers strung above it from a makeshift contraption that I seem to recall involved a coat-hanger. Then lots of buttered brown bread, nothing fancy, as nothing fancy goes in the Hebrides, with shots of whisky and coffee to follow. It was a late breakfast, so we were ravenous as opposed to just hungry, and the sight and smell of the fish grilling were mesmerising. So this is an ode to Charlie Boxer, author of that memory and fire-builder supreme.

You need a tripod set over a lively log fire, or you could rig something up with coat-hangers strung across as mentioned, anything really that provides the wherewithal to hang the fish. Secure these through the tail with some string, suspend them about six inches above the burning embers or logs, and cook until they are glistening with oil and warmed through – ideally they should be dripping. You are not seeking to cook them as such, it is more a question of bringing them back to life. One **kipper** will probably do for two people of relatively light appetite, a whole one each for more serious eaters. Dish them up with lots of **grainy brown bread** spread with **unsalted butter**. Accompany with **whisky** for the brave, and **coffee**.

Kit Tripod, string

CRISPY DUCK HASH

For 4 people

This falls at the glam end of the hash scale, employing a tub of duck rillettes. If you think how good potatoes roasted or fried in duck or goose fat are, this is passed on here, with the added pleasure of crispy little shreds of duck too. There is no need to peel your potatoes before cooking them, and the skin turns especially crispy. The idea is that you have potatoes for supper the night before and just cook up some extra with brunch in mind. It's good for any kind of rillettes or, more prosaically, corned beef, in which case you'll need a slug of oil.

1 x 200g tub of duck rillettes
2–3 shallots, peeled and finely chopped
8 small waxy potatoes, cooked and sliced
a couple of shakes of Tabasco (optional)

Melt the duck rillettes in a large non-stick frying pan over a medium heat, then add the shallots and potatoes and fry for about 20 minutes until golden and crispy. Turn them frequently, and season with Tabasco should you have some.

Short order

A little fruit goes so well with duck – pop a few halved plums (about 6 should do you) into the frying pan after you've removed the hash, and colour them on either side.

Kit Stove, frying pan, sharp knife, spatula

ALL-IN-ONE FRY-UP

For 4 people

Lay 8 rashers of **rindless streaky bacon** over the base of a large non-stick frying pan, or as many as will fit, and fry either side until a tad golden. Scatter over 4 small sliced **cooked potatoes**, add a handful of **sliced or button mushrooms** per person, drizzle over a little **vegetable or olive oil** and grind over some **black pepper**. Keep frying, stirring now and again, for 10–20 minutes, until everything is evenly golden and crispy. Make 4 wells in the mixture and break an **egg** into each one. Cook for 2–3 minutes, then turn using a spatula and cook for a moment longer to set the top, leaving the yolk runny.

Kit Stove, frying pan, spatula, sharp knife

HUCKLEBERRY FINN FRY-UP

For 4 people

There is a scene in Mark Twain's *The Adventures of Tom Sawyer* where the 'pirates' Tom, Joe and Huck go for an early morning dip and return to their camp 'wonderfully refreshed, glad-hearted, and ravenous'.

'They soon had the camp-fire blazing up again. While Joe was slicing bacon for breakfast, Tom and Huck asked him to hold on a minute; they stepped to a promising nook in the river bank and threw in their lines; almost immediately they had reward. Joe had not had time to get impatient before they were back again with some handsome bass, a couple of sun-perch and a small catfish – provision enough for quite a family. They fried the fish with the bacon and were astonished; for no fish had ever seemed so delicious before. They did not know that the quicker a fresh water fish is on the fire after he is caught the better he is; and they reflected a little upon what a sauce open air sleeping, open air exercise, bathing and a large ingredient of hunger makes, too.'

To this end, heat a slug of **vegetable or olive oil** in a large non-stick frying pan and fry a couple of handfuls of **lardons** (1 x 100g packet) until lightly golden. Add enough **mackerel or other fish fillets** for 4 people skin down to the pan, season them with **black pepper** and continue to fry until you can see they are almost cooked through. Flip them over and continue to cook briefly until the flesh is just firm. Dish up with lots of **buttered brown toast** (see pages 39–40).

Kit Stove, frying pan, spatula

SCRAMBLED OMELETTE

For 4 people

Halfway between an omelette and scrambled eggs, what the Spanish would call a *revueltos*, this is a delicious caddy for any number of seasonal ingredients, but here an excuse to indulge in lots of fondue-esque Swiss cheese and runny egg. A lovely supper with a tomato salad as well as a delicious meal at the start of the day.

Whisk 8 **medium eggs** with some **seasoning** in a bowl, and mix in a couple of handfuls of thinly sliced **fondue cheese** – Gruyère, Beaufort, Abondance and the like. Heat a large non-stick frying pan over a medium heat – any higher and the eggs will scramble instantly without the cheese melting, but a barbecue will be good after the first half hour or so of intense heat. Add a knob of **butter** (or a slug of **vegetable oil**) and, once the foam subsides, tip in the omelette mixture and fry it, folding it over a few times as it sets on the base, until the cheese is clearly melted but the last of the egg is still runny. Dish up straight away, with **hot buttered toast** (see pages 39–40).

Kit Stove or barbecue, mixing bowl, sharp knife, frying pan, spatula

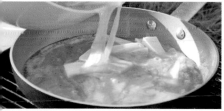

COWBOY BEANS ON TOAST

For 4–6 people

For a cheat's version of the real thing, it's cans. You can replace the lardons with thick slices of salami, adding them 5 minutes before the end, to make it even more 'ranch-hand'. If you have one of those choppers (see page 19), it can be usefully employed here to finely chop the onion, garlic, apple and tomatoes. I'd give the beans a rinse too, by refilling the drained cans with fresh water and draining them again.

a slug of vegetable or olive oil
a couple of handfuls of lardons (or 1 x 100g packet)
3 shallots, peeled and finely chopped
1 garlic clove, peeled and finely chopped
½ an apple, diced quite finely
1 x 400g can of chopped tomatoes
2 tomatoes, peeled and finely chopped
2 x 400g cans of haricot beans
2 teaspoons light muscovado sugar
1 teaspoon Dijon mustard
a pinch of chilli flakes or a few shakes of Tabasco
sea salt
butter (ideally salted) to serve

Heat a slug of oil in a large saucepan or casserole over a medium heat and fry the lardons until they are a light gold, then add the shallot, garlic and apple and continue to fry until glossy and softened. Add all the remaining ingredients and simmer, covered, for 15–20 minutes. Drop a few slivers of butter in the centre and leave to melt. Dish up with buttered toast (see pages 39–40).

Kit Stove or tripod, saucepan or casserole, sharp knife, can opener

HOT SMOKED SALMON ROLLS

A Glastonbury favourite, there are two routes here, one hedonistic and the other slightly less so. In the first you butter your baguette or rolls on the outside as well as the inside before cooking them, to achieve a seriously crisp and buttery crumb. The second route is to butter the inside only. For one or two people, rolls will do nicely, whereas for three upwards, baguettes in varying lengths will play to a crowd.

Either way fill them with **smoked salmon**, squeeze over a little **lemon juice** and grind over some **black pepper** in time-honoured fashion.

You then have two ways of cooking them. Either heat a frying pan over a medium heat for 5 minutes, wrap the rolls in foil and heat for 4–5 minutes each side. Alternatively, without wrapping the rolls, toast them for a couple of minutes either side on the grid of a hot barbecue. Napkins all round and go.

Kit Stove, frying pan or barbecue, foil

CUPPA TEA AND A PIECE OF CAKE

This chapter is arguably the cheat in the equation, as all these recipes are designed on a 'cook 'n' go' basis, something to whiz up before you leave home. Which is not to say that you can't bake cakes in your barbecue, your Dream-Pot or whatever ingenious outdoor equipment you are lugging with you, but why go to the trouble? Baking cakes is a messy business, best performed in a controlled oven with lots of running water and a dishwasher to hand. So bake and take seems by far the most practical solution.

Nothing fancy, mind you – rustic times call for rustic cakes. I am the first to immerse myself at home in the art of decoration, but sticky slicks of icing have a habit of attracting unwanted insects and finding their way into places in which you would rather not come across icing, especially after dark. So, with that in mind, here is a collection of unadorned old-fashioned favourites – a good chocolate sponge, a cherry loaf, a dense banana cake, flapjacks, a fudgy jam sandwich shortbread, or Breton gateau, a ginger cake and some chocolate chip cookies.

The ideal is either something that can be transported in its tin or wrapped in foil, and cut into squares or fingers, or a loaf cake, which is that much sturdier than a tiered round one. And flapjacks and cookies are ever transportable, good for handing round in the car while you're sitting in a traffic jam or on the quayside waiting for a ferry.

Which leads on to 'that' cuppa – rarely does a mug of tea taste quite as good as at the end of an afternoon spent making sandcastles on a windswept beach, or coming out of the drizzle from a clifftop walk. But it has to be builder's, a good strong brew like Yorkshire or Barry's; I'd rather save the elegance of Darjeeling and white tea for that long soak in a bubble bath that I'm looking forward to when I get home.

And it's teabags, which doesn't mean forgoing the teapot. I find it hard to live without my little Brown Betty, and the temptation is to tuck it in between all the other paraphernalia in the boot of the car, but an enamel teapot is guaranteed to scrub up well whatever abuses you put it through, and can't break. Back to the teabags: I reckon you can get a fine brew if you follow the usual procedure of warming the pot first, and always steep a minimum of two bags – somehow one bag just doesn't do it.

But I feel I've failed you on the milk. I had hoped that in the interim years since I went caravanning as a child something new would have appeared on the market and cold-shouldered UHT and dried skimmed milk powder, ever the stuff of canteens and railway cars, but sadly not. And of the two, I'd rather the latter. If you only want enough fresh milk for tea and coffee and lugging a pint around seems de trop, you can use the small aluminium bottles that come in travel sizes (see page 18), or small empty juice bottles.

CHOCOLATE CAMPING CAKE

Enough for several days, or 9 big squares

Brownie-like in its charm, and exceptionally gooey,
so the only way to transport it is in its tin.

200g unsalted butter, softened
200g golden caster sugar
3 medium eggs
100g ground almonds
100g plain flour
25g cocoa powder, sifted
2 teaspoons baking powder, sifted
2 tablespoons dark rum
100g dark chocolate chips

Preheat the oven to 170°C fan/190°C/
gas mark 5 and butter a 23cm square
cake tin. Place the butter, sugar, eggs,
ground almonds, flour, cocoa and
baking powder in the bowl of a food
processor and cream together, then
add the rum. Transfer the mixture to
a bowl and fold in two-thirds of the
chocolate chips.

Spoon the cake mixture into the prepared tin, smoothing the surface, and
scatter over the remaining chocolate
chips. Bake for 30–40 minutes, until
it feels dry and firm in the centre and
a skewer inserted comes out clean.
Run a knife around the edge and leave
to cool. Wrap foil around the tin to
transport, otherwise it can be cut into
quarters and stacked with paper or
plastic in between the layers.

CHERRY TEA LOAF

Makes a good-sized loaf cake

A classically elegant old-fashioned teatime loaf with a Madeira-style crumb. Ideally you want the dark red undyed cherries here, but the poppy red cocktail ones will do too.

65g unsalted butter, melted and cooled
4 medium eggs
200g golden caster sugar
1 teaspoon vanilla extract
100ml double cream
200g plain flour
1 heaped teaspoon baking powder
3 tablespoons smooth orange juice
125g whole glacé cherries
icing sugar for sifting

Preheat the oven to 170°C fan/190°C/gas mark 5. Brush the inside of a 22cm/1.3 litre loaf tin with a little of the melted butter. Unless your tin has a non-stick coating, line the base with baking parchment. Whisk the eggs and sugar together in a bowl, then add the vanilla extract and cream. Sift the flour and baking powder together and gradually fold in. Finally stir in the rest of the melted butter and the orange juice, and fold in half the cherries. Pour the mixture into the cake tin and scatter over the remaining cherries, which will sink as the cake bakes. Bake for 45–50 minutes, until the cake is golden and risen, the top feels completely dry and a skewer inserted into the centre comes out clean. Leave to cool for 10–15 minutes, then run a knife around the edge of the tin, turn the cake on to a wire rack the right way up and leave to cool. Dust with icing sugar. The cake will keep well wrapped in foil or in an airtight container for several days.

TWICE-BAKED BANANA CAKE

Enough for several days, or 9 big squares

This takes its inspiration from the Flour Power City Bakery's twice-baked banana cake. Made in a brownie tin, it's turned out, smothered in frangipan and then popped back into the oven to give it a lovely gooey top. It's really important that your bananas are ripe, blackening in patches – no problem for those who tend to overstock the fruit bowl, but otherwise worth planning in advance.

Cake
225g unsalted butter, softened
225g golden caster sugar
3 medium eggs
300g plain flour
1 tablespoon baking powder, sifted
4 tablespoons dark rum
1 teaspoon vanilla extract
3 good-sized over-ripe bananas, peeled and mashed
120g raisins

Frangipan
125g ground almonds
75g unsalted butter, softened
100g golden caster sugar
1 medium egg, plus 1 egg white

Preheat the oven to 180°C fan/200°C/gas mark 6. Butter a 23cm square baking tin (i.e. a brownie tin), line the base with greaseproof paper and then butter this too. Cream the butter and sugar together in a food processor, then incorporate the eggs, then the flour and baking powder, and finally the rum and vanilla. Scoop the cake mixture into a large bowl and mix in the bananas and raisins. Transfer the cake mixture to the prepared tin, smoothing the surface, and bake for 40–50 minutes, until the cake is firm and risen and a skewer inserted into the centre comes out clean.

Line a baking tray with a sheet of greaseproof paper. Run a knife around the edge of the cake, invert it on to the paper, then remove the base paper from the cake itself. Now leave for about 5 minutes to settle while you make the frangipan.

Whiz all the ingredients for the frangipan in a food processor until smooth and creamy. Spread over the surface of the cake (i.e. the upturned base), taking it almost to the edge; it will trickle down as it bakes. Return the cake to the oven for 15–25 minutes, until lightly golden. Leave to cool, then slip the cake on to a new sheet of baking paper or foil large enough to envelop it. Wrap it up – I normally tie it with string, which makes it easy to carry. It should be good for several days. It's also amenable to being cut into halves or quarters, and is relatively sturdy, should it prove easier to transport in this fashion. And as ever, it can be stored in an airtight container.

GINGER CAKE

Makes 8 generous wedges

My son recently came across a copy of what was my favourite cookery book at his age, *The Pooh Cook Book*, with recipes by Katie Stewart, and I couldn't resist making the honey cake I remembered as being especially good. It's still delicious, and I've upped the ginger in the interests of the raspberry sauce, with which it features in the Famous Five High Teas chapter (see page 76). Don't worry if it seems to sink a little in the centre – many of the best cakes do, and it'll still be suitably fluffy. But if this really worries you, bake it in a 23cm brownie tin for 30–35 minutes instead.

150g unsalted butter
125g light muscovado sugar
180g set honey
2 medium eggs
200g plain flour
2 teaspoons baking powder
2 teaspoons ground ginger
a pinch of sea salt

Preheat the oven to 170°C fan/190°C/gas mark 5, and butter and line the base of a 20cm cake tin with a removable base. Gently heat the butter, sugar and honey in a small saucepan until melted and leave to cool for about 10 minutes. Beat in the eggs, then sift over and fold in the flour, baking powder and ginger, and add the salt. Pour into the prepared tin, give it a couple of sharp taps to bring up any air bubbles, and bake for 35–40 minutes, until a skewer inserted into the centre comes out clean. Leave to cool, then remove the collar and the base paper and either wrap in foil or store in an airtight container. It is a cake that keeps well for some days, getting stickier as it goes.

JAM SANDWICH SHORTBREAD

Makes 8 generous wedges

This is a Breton speciality, a deliciously cakey shortbread-type cake with a gooey heart of strawberry jam, the secret of its success being the salty butter.

225g self-raising flour, sifted
110g golden caster sugar
110g icing sugar, sifted
225g lightly salted butter, diced*
5 medium egg yolks
¾ teaspoon vanilla extract
125g jam (wild strawberry, fruits of the forest, etc.)
1 egg yolk, blended with 1 teaspoon water

Place the flour, both sugars and the butter in the bowl of a food processor and whiz until the mixture is crumb-like. Blend the egg yolks with the vanilla in a bowl, then add to the dry ingredients and whiz to a soft, sticky dough. Wrap this in clingfilm and chill for at least a couple of hours.

Preheat the oven to 170°C fan/190°C/gas mark 5, and butter a 20cm cake tin at least 5cm deep with a removable base. Press half the dough into the tin, laying a sheet of clingfilm over the top and smoothing it with your fingers, then remove this. Work the jam in a bowl to loosen it, and spread this over the surface to within 1cm of the rim. Roll out the remainder of the dough on a well-floured work surface (it will still be quite sticky) into a circle fractionally larger than the cake tin. Lay this on top of the jam and press it into place, tidying the edges using your fingers. Liberally paint the surface with the egg wash, and make a lattice pattern using the tines of a fork. Bake for about 45 minutes, until deeply golden, crusty and risen. Run a knife around the collar and leave to cool (it will sink in the middle), then remove the collar. This cake will keep well for several days in an airtight container. Serve cut into wedges.

*If using a Breton salted butter, use half and half with unsalted.

CHOCOLATE CHIP COOKIES

Makes 20–25

A small reminder of the comfort of a home kitchen, and a great negotiating tool to use with fractious children.

vegetable oil for brushing
110g lightly salted butter, diced
75g golden caster sugar
50g light muscovado sugar
1 medium egg
½ teaspoon vanilla extract
150g plain flour
1 teaspoon baking powder
50g raisins
150g dark chocolate (approx. 70% cocoa solids), chopped

Preheat the oven to 170°C fan/190°C/gas mark 5 and lightly oil 2 or 3 baking trays. Cream the butter and both sugars together in a food processor, then incorporate the egg and vanilla. Sift the flour and baking powder and mix in. Transfer the mixture to a large bowl and mix in the raisins and chopped chocolate. Drop heaped teaspoons of the mixture in mounds on to the trays, spaced well apart. Bake for 12–15 minutes, until pale gold all over but slightly darker around the edges. Loosen the cookies straight away by carefully slipping a spatula underneath, then leave them to cool – you can transfer them to a wire rack after a few minutes if you wish. They are at their best the day they are made, but are still in good form the day after.

DELICIOUSLY CHEWY FLAPJACKS

Enough for several teas

A good no-frills classic flapjack, this has two lives, one for tea (great for the journey), and at a later date it will stand in as a crumble topping for whatever soft fruits you're warming on the grill (see page 161). And, as porridge is one of the last things you should be thinking of making while you're away, it's nice to get some oats in, processed ones rather than anything too hearty and butch – the flapjacks should have a 'soft' side to their character.

240g lightly salted butter, diced
180g demerara sugar
6 tablespoons golden syrup
350g rolled oats

Preheat the oven to 160°C fan/180°C/gas mark 4. Gently melt the butter with the sugar and golden syrup in a medium-sized saucepan over a medium heat. Stir in the rolled oats. Tip the mixture into a 23cm square tin or one that's equivalent in size, pressing it down, and bake for 20–25 minutes. Leave to cool and then cut into squares or fingers. Transport wrapped in foil or in an airtight container.

FAMOUS FIVE HIGH TEAS

'I know what we'll do this hols! We'll hire a caravan and go off in it by ourselves. Do let's! Oh, do let's!'

God, what fun. I was a Blyton junkie as a child, and could happily consume a book a day between breakfast and lunch – for which I count myself lucky, as in my husband's household Blyton novellas were forbidden. Even though she is no longer the middle-class bête noire that she once was, I find it ironic that Enid Blyton is possibly best remembered for her fine food writing. Rarely do you hear her praised for her erudite passages about smugglers and secret tunnels, but get any seasoned Blyton reader on to the subject of 'those picnics' and they mist over with nostalgia at the thought of hard-boiled eggs dipped in salt, cake and raspberry sauce, tomato and potted meat sandwiches and the gallons of ginger beer that washed it all down.

In *Five Go Off in a Caravan*, she doesn't disappoint. There is feast after feast after feast, until you get to Chapter 11, 'Fun at the Circus Camp', which kicks off with a gluttonous orgy, with Anne clearing up the breakfast things while Dick goes off to the farm to stock up for the next meal. The farmer's wife shows him 'two big baskets full of delicious food. Slices of ham I've cured myself', 'and a pot of brawn I've made. And some fresh lettuces and radishes I pulled myself this morning early. And some more tomatoes.'

'"How gorgeous!" said Dick, eyeing the food in delight. "What's in the other basket?"

"Eggs, butter, milk, and a tin of shortbread I've baked."' She even slips a few homemade sweets into the basket as a parting shot.

While earlier in the book, Anne, who adopts the role of mini-mummy, says, 'I've got eggs and tomatoes and potted meat, and plenty of bread, and cake we bought today, and a pound of butter.' A pound of butter? They go shopping again the next day, for heaven's sake. I've come to the conclusion, given that this was written in 1946, when post-war rationing was still in place and ingredients like butter, eggs and bacon were thin on the ground, that all these feasts were Blyton's fantasies of the way life should be, after years of wartime hardship.

But they are one of the best aspects of her books: the level of appetite that she conveys, and satisfying it, in a way that is central to life out of doors, is something she captures perfectly. In our coddled, environmentally controlled daily routines, so often we eat because it is time to eat without truly experiencing the hunger that is so enjoyably sated when you are 'ravenous'. So let us raise a boiled egg to Blyton, dip it in salt and salute the delicious innocence of the Five's picnic teas.

'Nobby went to help Anne. Together they boiled ten eggs hard in the little saucepan. Then Anne made tomato sandwiches with potted meat and got out the cake the farmer's wife had given them. She remembered the raspberry syrup, too – how lovely!

Soon they were all sitting on the rocky ledge which was still warm, watching the sun go down into the lake. It was the most beautiful evening, with the lake as blue as a cornflower and the sky flecked with rosy clouds. They held their hard-boiled eggs in one hand and a piece of bread and butter in the other, munching happily. There was a dish of salt for everyone to dip their eggs into.

"I don't know why, but the meals we have on picnics always taste so much nicer than the ones we have indoors," said George. "For instance, even if we had hard-boiled eggs and bread and butter indoors, they wouldn't taste as nice as these."

"Can everyone eat two eggs?" asked Anne. "I did two each. And there's plenty of cake – and more sandwiches and some plums we picked this morning."

"Best meal I've ever had in my life," said Nobby, and picked up his second egg.'

MENU

One of the best parts of this tea is that there is very, very little in the way of preparation, as well there might be, given the age of those preparing it. So gather it all together, or even let your offspring do this, and send them off with a basket and a rug to a shore beside a lake or a grassy dune, while you settle down to a decent book. And if they're full at this time of the day, it also allows you to bump supper a little later into the evening and indulge in a slow-cooked one-pot dish that simmers away for a couple of hours.

HARD-BOILED EGGS WITH SALT

I like boiled **eggs** that are a touch runny within, to which end boil them for 6–7 minutes. But if you want them 'hard-boiled' in the literal sense, boil them for 10 minutes. Either way, drain and refill the pan with cold water. Any leftovers can be turned into Devilled Eggs (see page 89). Serve with a small bowl of **salt**.

Kit Stove, saucepan

GINGER CAKE WITH RASPBERRY SAUCE

For the raspberry sauce, fold a couple of large handfuls of **raspberries** into 4–5 tablespoons of **raspberry jam** in a jar. Serve this spooned over wedges of **Ginger Cake** (see page 65).

CURRANT BUNS

Spread **curranty buns** with **butter** and quarter. Unsalted butter please (even though travelling back in time it would almost certainly have been salted) – the sweet lactic butters of the Continent are hugely superior with currant buns.

POTTED MEAT AND TOMATO SANDWICHES

Potted meat in the 1940s would normally have implied chopped meat preserved in butter, which seems on the sophisticated side for a bunch of children for high tea, though given Blyton's love of butter, perhaps this is exactly what she intended. Or it might have been corned beef, or liver sausage perhaps, which, together with tomatoes, made up one of my favourite after-school sandwiches as a child, especially when eaten sitting on the grass after a swim wrapped in a towel, my idea of heaven. These days, I tend to interpret potted meat as being some silky little pâté or other. Sandwiches filled with peppery mounds of mustard and cress and sticky jam sandwiches hold the same charm.

You also want **plums** and plenty of **ginger beer**.

UNEXPECTED GUESTS FOR DRINKS

The title of this chapter could have a double entendre, so perhaps I should establish that it is the 'welcome' kind of guest to whom I refer. The last time we went camping *en famille* on our little sailing boat, *Winkle*, we took time early afternoon to *reconnoitre* the best spots along the river where we might be able to moor and set up a small tent beside the boat, as we knew from experience that on a fine Saturday these tend to get nabbed long before sundown.

Having settled in and cooked a delicious supper of Roast Lamb with Sweet and Sour Tomato Sauce (see page 127) and a warming pot of Tumbet (see page 103), we attempted a game of mah-jong, quickly abandoned when we discovered that it is a game best played on a large dining table, and therefore settled to bed rather earlier than usual. I think we managed two hours' sleep before there was a loud 'ker-splosh' on the water as a squadron of Canada geese skidded along the surface, grinding to a halt just beside us. I thought birds were meant to go to sleep at night, but they continued to take off and land, honking loudly, as though practising some wartime manoeuvre under the cover of darkness, all night long. Didn't sleep a wink.

Pity for the wealthy isn't a sentiment that tends to reverberate round family tents, but I did feel quite sorry for the owners of the faux-Georgian pile fronting the river on the opposite bank if these 'guests' were regulars, and imagined how they must have felt on their first night in their beautiful new home. That's one of the good things about camping – you can move on.

Any case, returning to guests of the welcome kind, I mean those old friends game enough to pop in and spend a couple of hours 'camping' with you, or the new friends you make – the camaraderie, the way that all ages find themselves with a whole set of new acquaintances after a week in the wild, is one of the warming aspects of camping. So this

chapter is about suggestions for little snacks, readily whipped up in such emergencies. Actually it's quite good for when you're at home too – why wait to go camping to cheat?

SALTED POPCORN

Good for 4–6 people

Popcorn takes up so little space in its unpopped form, and it's a great child bonder – give 'em a big bowl of corn and send 'em on their way to sort out the woes of the world together. It's also now officially recognised as a health food, so we should be eating lots and lots of it. On the washing-up front, it should leave you with a completely clean pan that calls for no more than a wipe with kitchen paper once it's cooled down.

Heat a thread of **vegetable oil** (olive is fine if that's all you have with you) in a medium to large saucepan over a gentle heat, scatter over a single layer of **popcorn** and cover. After about 5 minutes you should find that the occasional pop starts to crescendo into a full-on firework display. So hold tight with the lid, giving the pan the odd shake and once it dies down a minute or so later, remove it from the heat, even if you're still getting the occasional pop. Either spoon the popcorn into a plastic bag or leave it in the pan, sprinkle over a little **fine salt**, tie or cover and give it a good shake.

Kit Stove, saucepan

CRISPS 'N' DIP

Makes a small tub's worth

If you take one of those oh-so-useful tubs of dip from the chill counter camping with you, I know from experience the mess that tends to happen when you pop the half-finished tub back into the chill-box. Better to start from scratch and pack some Boursin.

Scoop a packet of **Boursin** (usually 150g) into a bowl and add **milk** a few drops at a time, blending it with the cheese, until you have a dippable dip. Add **lemon juice** to taste, and dish it up with a big bag of rustic crisps or **tortilla chips**, or with some **radishes** or other crudités.

FETA WITH PISTACHIOS IN HONEY

For 6 people

Feta makes a good travelling companion: its shape, texture and the fact that it comes hermetically sealed all make it a goer in the chill-box. But more than that, I love this combination of the salty creamy cheese with the sweetness of honey, and although it's lovely to chip away at with a glass of wine before dinner, it will also stand in as a small sweet-come-savoury at the other end of it.

a couple of handfuls of pistachios
runny honey
1 x 200g slab of feta cheese

Combine the pistachios with a couple of tablespoons of honey in a bowl, adding just enough to coat and hold them together. Spread these over the feta on a plate, drizzle over a little more honey and dig in with a knife, to help pile it on to whatever crispies you're eating with it.

To eat
Sardinian wafer breads such as carta di musica and pane carasau are packable and deliciously elegant, but any little cracker will do here, as will very crispy toast.

SQUASHED FLY BISCUITS AND CHEESE

In *Swallows and Amazons* the natives fare almost as well as the Famous Five on the feasting front, with a birthday hamper groaning with goodies:

'a birthday cake, a huge one with Victoria written in pink sugar on the white icing and two large cherries in the middle. Then there was a cold chicken. Then there was a salad in a big pudding-basin. Then there was an enormous gooseberry tart. Then there was a melon.

Then there were more ordinary stores, a tin of golden syrup, two big pots of marmalade and a great tin of squashed-fly biscuits. Squashed-fly biscuits are those flat biscuits with currants in them, just the thing for explorers.'

I'm so glad that Arthur Ransome took the trouble to describe these biscuits, because I was agonising over how to introduce the subject. A few years after he wrote this book, my parents-in-law were holidaying in the South of France, according to my mother-in-law in 'rather a grotty villa', with a great friend who handled the PR for Aristotle Onassis. The night before they were due to leave, a telephone call came through informing their friend that Onassis had just arrived in the harbour on his yacht and thought he might 'pop in' for a drink, which threw the assembled company into complete panic. The cupboard was bare, as was the fridge, save for a chunk of Cheddar and a packet of Garibaldi biscuits that my mother-in-law had picked up from a corner shop on the way back from the beach in anticipation of midnight hunger.

Et voilà the solution – **squashed fly biscuits** broken into pieces with fine slivers of **Cheddar** on top. My mother-in-law has always put the success of these little eats down as the reason Onassis insisted they join him on his yacht for a few days and whisked them off to Portofino. So, next time you're eyeing up someone's Winnebago or VW Combi along the 'theirs looks drier/comfier than mine' lines – whip out those Garibaldi biscuits, and you never know where it might lead to.

CHEESE AND HAM PINWHEELS

Makes 6–8 bites

Knocked up in a jiffy, these can also be assembled well in advance and heated to order. You can toast them on the barbecue, should you have it lit, as well as in a frying pan on a stove, again for a few minutes each side.

Trim the edges of a **tortilla wrap** to the diameter of the base of your frying pan. Cover the tortilla with thinly sliced **roast ham**, lay some diced **medium-mature Cheddar** in a line about a third of the way in from the edge, then roll up into a torpedo. Wrap this in foil, twisting the ends like a cracker, and slice off any excess, leaving the ends sealed.

Heat a large frying pan over a low heat for 5 minutes, then heat the torpedo for 3–4 minutes each side. Unwrap, slice diagonally into little appetisers, and pass round straight away.

Kit Barbecue, or stove and frying pan, foil, sharp knife

ZAHTAR PITTAS

Zahtar is a spicy blend of dried thyme, sesame seeds and sumac, a tart red berry that grows wild in the moutains of Lebanon. It's a great little dried seasoning that can be sprinkled over toast and flatbreads drizzled with oil, and it is worth ordering a small pouch if you're buying in your spice blends (see page 28).

Warm some **pitta breads**, either over the barbecue or in a frying pan on a stove. Slit them open, drizzle some **extra virgin olive oil** over the cut surfaces, scatter with **zahtar** and either serve as little pizzettas or slice into thick strips to serve as finger food.

Kit Barbecue, or stove and frying pan

HUMMUS

For 4 people

A tin of chickpeas is instantly whisked into a rustic hummus with the two essentials of Camping Marinade and a little Middle Eastern Spice Blend.

Drain a 400g tin of **chickpeas** (ideally give them a rinse by refilling the tin with water and draining them again) and coarsely mash in a bowl with 4 tablespoons of **Camping Marinade** (see page 27), ½ teaspoon of **Middle Eastern Spice Blend** (see page 29) and a little salt, using a fork. Don't worry if some chickpeas remain whole, it adds to the charm. Pile on to a small plate, drizzle over a little **extra virgin olive oil** and dust with a little more of the spice.

A KIND OF GUACAMOLE

For 4 people

Skin 2 **avocados** and mash them in a bowl with 3 tablespoons of **Camping Marinade** (see page 27), a little salt, and, if you like, about $1/3$ of a teaspoon of **Middle Eastern Spice Blend** (see page 29). Pile on to a small plate, scatter with slivers of **cherry tomato**, and drizzle over a little **extra virgin olive oil**.

Kit Sharp knife

To eat
Dish either of these dips up with corn chips or warm pittas, or spin them out into something more substantial with oily black olives and sun-dried tomatoes in oil, or salami.

CRAB PÂTÉ

For 6 people

A great cheat – we all know how prohibitively expensive crab can be, but it's the brown meat that has the most flavour, something Shippam's have long made a virtue of with their spread, which can be eked out into a silky little pâté with lots of butter. Dish up with a plate of thin slices of baguette, which you can always toast first if you've got the barbecue on the go. Crackers are good too.

Blend a couple of 75g jars of **crab paste** (e.g. Shippam's) in a bowl with half as much **softened unsalted butter**, a drizzle of **lemon juice**, and a little **cayenne pepper** and **salt**.

SARDINE PÂTÉ

For 4 people

Go for a tinned sardine with a little pedigree here, something they do especially well in the environs of Brittany. Scoop this up with toast, crackers or bread. It's also good with celery and radishes.

Work 2 generous slices of **softened unsalted butter** in a bowl, i.e. about a quarter of a 250g packet. Add the fillets from 3 **tins of sardines** and mash them together. Blend in 1 tablespoon of **Camping Marinade** (see page 27) and a little **salt**. Spread on a small plate and scatter over a little chopped **parsley**.

DEVILLED EGGS

For 4 people

However good hard-boiled eggs dipped in salt are, there is a fair chance that your offspring will return from their 'Famous Five' tea clean of Ginger Cake and Raspberry Sauce, but with only one less egg than when they set out. The leftovers can be shelled and dipped into a spicy mayo or for the full retro experience, you could cut them open, spoon the mayo on top and dust over a little more spice. You could also mash any leftover eggs with the spice blend and mayo and use to fill sandwiches. In this case, discard the egg white at the wider end of a couple of the eggs to render it yolk rich.

Blend ¼ teaspoon of **Middle Eastern Spice Blend** (see page 29) with 4 tablespoons of **mayonnaise**. This is enough for about 4 **eggs**.

Kit Stove, saucepan, sharp knife

Other good things for emergencies

Olives: Ideally in pouches, which are more convenient than jars and lighter to carry.

Salami: Invest in a whole one for hacking away at with your pocket knife. This is a stable product that won't come to any harm out of the fridge, the worst scenario being that the top slice may dry out.

Salted cashews: They take up less space than crisps.

Breadsticks: Ideally artisanal – great for when you don't have fresh bread for dipping.

Cherry tomatoes: Will turn a dip or two, with some bread, into a light supper.

ONE-POTS

An abiding memory of one-pot cooking out of doors is of visiting a market in the Ourika Valley in Morocco early one morning. On the approach along a pot-holed mountain road, at a distance we could see plumes of smoke gently rising into the air at intervals. As we got closer this took shape as a line of tagines simmering away over open fires at the roadside. The stall-holders would arrive at dawn and, before setting out their wares, would mix up some meat and vegetables with spices and water and leave it to simmer for several hours while they set to work. The results were tantalising – I longed to join them at their upturned crates and dip a piece of flatbread into the soupy juices, as they were doing.

At home, we layer sophistication into our casseroles by building them up in stages, gently sweating different vegetables and herbs, searing the meat, reducing the wine and so forth. But look to other cultures and it becomes clear just how good a very basic casserole can be. One-pot dishes are by nature the simplest and potentially the most humble of repasts, and when camping the most important consideration is the washing up, given the paucity of water, so it makes sense to plan any meal backwards from the tail end. But I have taken them further than that, by taking a leaf out of those Moroccan pedlars' cookery books and abandoning all the usual formalities completely. The stews, even when taking inspiration from Italy or mythical cowboys out West, are 'put-it-all-in-a-pot-and-go'. And it is surprising how little they lack. I am not suggesting that they are necessarily what you would choose to dish up at your next dinner party (although I have done that), but they suit the mood and the occasion.

On a practical note, this isn't simply to allow us to indulge our inner slob, although that does come into it. Cooking over an open fire, be it in a cast-iron casserole suspended on a tripod or sitting on a trivet, calls for arms of asbestos when it comes to stirring the dish. I am none too keen on hanging over a hissing gas ring either. So the idea is that you can assemble these completely in advance of cooking them, save for very occasionally having to fry an onion. The one proviso that I should, of course, be banging on about is to ensure you use good-quality ingredients. But with all the time in the world to rootle out lovely hidden farm shops, there is no reason why this shouldn't be the case. Shopping for food tends to come top of my list whatever the holiday, and more than ever if I am camping.

NO-CHOP SPAGHETTI PUTTANESCA

For 4 people

As our stock spaghetti dish at home, this remains in the comfort zone when away – it's the camping version, bung it all in a pan and leave to simmer. A little Parmesan is optional here – but unless the perfectionist in you got the upper hand when packing you're probably not going to have a grater. Finely sliced?

4 handfuls of spaghetti

Sauce
3 tablespoons extra virgin olive oil
½ teaspoon crushed garlic
6 salted anchovy fillets
1 x 400g can of chopped tomatoes
¼ teaspoon crushed dried red chillies
1 heaped tablespoon capers
4 tablespoons sliced green olives
sea salt

If you are reliant on one ring, the sauce can be made in advance and reheated. Heat the olive oil in a medium saucepan, add the garlic and anchovies and cook for a minute, mashing the anchovies into a paste. Add all the remaining sauce ingredients and simmer for 10–15 minutes, until glossy and thickened.

Boil the spaghetti in plenty of salted water until just tender, then drain it, return it to the pan and toss with the hot sauce.

Kit Stove, 2 saucepans

JACQUES TATI SOUP

For 4–6 people

The first day we took our little sailing boat on a jaunt down the River
Thames, we thought we would break ourselves in gently with 'a day's
camping'. So we meandered and moored in a lovely spot, and I set to
cooking this simple Syrian grain soup, a recipe given to me by a friend, the
cookery writer Nada Saleh.

As I was trying to get to grips with my one ring on the bank, and the fact
that I was not cooking with gas, I was cooking with meths, there was a
crack on the boat beside me, followed by an 'oops', then a 'blimey', and an
'OK guys, I need help.'

While I was preparing lunch my husband had been having a tinker with
the outboard, which had sheared clean away from the transom attaching
it to the boat. He had been left carrying the full weight of this iron beast
when he realised that the back of the boat was drifting out from the shore.

Normally very handy at such times, he could but shout orders, of which
I will spare you the detail, until, that is, we got to: 'I can't hold it, I can't
hold it, DO SOMETHING.'

I was trying: I had got back on to the boat, and I now leapt on to the shore
(as he had one foot on the boat and another on the shore and was doing
the splits in a fashion that would impress any ballerina) and held him
around the waist.

'Don't worry,' I said, 'I've got you.'

Uttering some endearment he fell into the Thames and disappeared
beneath the rippling water, heroically clutching the engine.

Mentally I rehearsed the life-saving moves practised so many years ago
in Woking swimming baths, and was dreading having to put them into
practice, so I was weak with relief when he bobbed to the surface, still
clutching the engine, baptised by the River Thames.

The moral of this is that, clearly, the boat hadn't been properly tied up in the first place. By whom?

I returned to preparing this soup, a glamorised version of the penitential rice soup they used to serve us every Friday at a Catholic convent I attended for a time in Belgium as a child, where curiously you were also given a glass of beer with every lunch, from the age of five. That may not sound like much of a recommendation, but actually it's delicious – and it is those little secular touches that go to make it in any case, the generous dousing with olive oil and lemon juice, some crusty bread and olives. Nada normally makes it with water, though I like to sneak in a little chicken stock cube or some Marigold Swiss Vegetable Bouillon Powder to give it a boost.

extra virgin olive oil
1 onion, peeled, halved and finely sliced
1 level teaspoon Middle Eastern Spice Blend (see page 29)
$^1/_3$ tin mug of green lentils
$^1/_3$ tin mug of basmati rice
$^1/_3$ tin mug of bulgar wheat
sea salt
lemon juice

Heat a slug of oil in a medium or large saucepan and fry the onion over a moderate flame until golden. Stir in the spice blend, then add the lentils, rice and bulgar. Add 5 tin mugs of water and a stock cube or powder if wished (see intro) and some salt. Bring to the boil, skim any foam from the surface, then half cover with a lid and simmer for 20 minutes, or until the grains are tender. Dish up with some olive oil poured over and a squeeze of lemon juice.

Kit Stove, saucepan, sharp knife

FRANKFURTER GOULASH

For 4 people

Variation on the theme of bangers and mash, and not dissimilar to Dublin coddle. Frankfurters are great camping material, as they don't require any grilling or frying. This is real soul food, the sort of dish any ravenous herdsman would welcome at the end of a dusty day.

½ tin mug of unsmoked bacon lardons (1 x 100g packet)
3 large onions, peeled, halved and sliced
8 medium waxy potatoes, scrubbed or peeled
12 frankfurter sausages
a couple of bay leaves
sea salt and black pepper
1 tin mug of chicken stock

Heat a large saucepan or casserole over a medium heat, add the lardons and fry in the rendered fat until golden. Add the onions and continue to fry, stirring frequently, until caramelised. Add the potatoes, frankfurters, bay leaves and some seasoning and gently mix. Pour over the chicken stock and gently simmer, covered, for 30–45 minutes, or until the potatoes are tender and sitting in a rich gravy – but keep an eye on it towards the end to make sure it doesn't cook dry.

Kit Stove or tripod, saucepan or casserole

MY BIG FAT CHILLI CON CARNE

For 6 people

It was my brother, a veteran camper, who told me how some friend of his had cooked up chilli with rice in a big cast-iron pot on a camping trip for five families, effortlessly, and I thought 'what a great idea'. And it takes an excuse like camping to dust off this period piece, which we seem to have resigned to the attic at home. It's ever good with guacamole (see page 86), or a lively avocado salad.

2 tablespoons vegetable oil
2 onions, peeled and finely chopped
1 teaspoon crushed garlic
2 teaspoons Middle Eastern Spice Blend (see page 29)
700g minced beef
2 x 400g cans of chopped tomatoes
1 tablespoon tomato purée
1 teaspoon fines herbes or herbes de Provence (optional)
sea salt
1 x 400g can of kidney beans, drained
savoury rice (see page 151), and, if you like, guacamole (see page 86), sour cream or
     fromage blanc and tortillas

Heat the oil in a large saucepan or casserole over a medium heat and fry the onions until a mid gold (10–15 minutes) giving them a lazy stir now and again, and adding the garlic just before you get there. Stir in the spice blend and the mince, turn up the heat and continue to cook until it changes colour, giving it the odd stir.

Add the chopped tomatoes, tomato purée, fines herbes or herbes de Provence if including, and some salt, then bring to a simmer and cook over a low heat for about an hour, adding the beans halfway through.

Dish up with an equally big pot of savoury rice, guacamole if you're aiming at fine dining, and I guess you could also run to sour cream and warmed tortillas.

Kit Stove or tripod, saucepan or casserole

LAMB, BARLEY AND ROSEMARY HOTPOT

For 6 people

Just a few adaptations to make this favourite camping-friendly. First, there is no real need to peel the potatoes, or the carrots, and assuming these are the smallest Chantenay type, they won't need cutting up either. In fact, the skin gives the broth a delicious savour. Nor is there any need to slice the meat – it cooks down to fork-tenderness and can be pulled apart once it's cooked. When at home, to avoid biting on bitter rosemary needles once the stew is cooked, I normally wrap the sprig in a small square of muslin, something you are very unlikely to have on hand in a field kitchen. But cut off the top of a teabag and empty out the tea, pop the rosemary inside and fold the top down, and problem sorted.

800g–1kg lamb neck fillet
3 onions, peeled, halved and thinly sliced
½ tin mug of pearl barley*
sea salt and black pepper
1 sprig of fresh rosemary
2 chicken stock cubes
2 tin mugs of small Chantenay carrots
6 small waxy potatoes, scrubbed or peeled as necessary, and halved or quartered lengthways
coarsely chopped fresh flat-leaf parsley to serve

Layer the lamb, onions and barley in a large saucepan or casserole, seasoning the ingredients as you go, and tucking in the rosemary. Pour over 4 mugs of water, filling the mug to where you would normally fill it for a cup of tea, crumble in the stock cubes, and press the ingredients down to submerge them. Bring to the boil and skim off any foam on the surface, then cover and cook over a low heat for 1 hour. Stir in the carrots and potatoes and cook for another 30 minutes. Taste for seasoning, and serve scattered with chopped parsley. The stew can also be made in advance and reheated.

* You can also use pearled spelt in lieu of the barley, in which case add it after the first 30 minutes of cooking.

Kit Stove or tripod, saucepan or casserole, sharp knife

MUSSEL POT

This makes for great communal eating, and a beach is just about the perfect place, where the mussels can either be cooked on a tripod or in a large pan over a portable gas stove.

Allow about 500g of **mussels** per person, and wash and pick them over in the usual fashion, pulling off the beards and discarding any that don't close when sharply tapped. Bring a glass of **white wine** to the boil with a few finely chopped **shallots** in a large saucepan or casserole, add the mussels, cover, and steam them open for 5 minutes or so, stirring or shaking the pan halfway through.

Kit Stove or tripod, saucepan or casserole

TUMBET

For 6 people

This Majorcan vegetable dish is very similar to ratatouille, but there is little in the way of frying involved except for the aubergines, which always taste on the strange side unless they are shown a hot pan with a little oil. But the winning trick is the potatoes – so good with the soupy tomato juices – which do away with the need to provide them separately. This is lovely with most offerings from the grill (see page 111), or, for those who don't eat meat, with some grilled goat's cheese perhaps.

extra virgin olive oil
1 large aubergine, trimmed and cut into chunks
2 onions, peeled and cut into slim wedges
5 medium waxy potatoes, thickly sliced
2 red peppers, core and seeds removed, cut into wide strips
2 courgettes, ends removed, thickly sliced
6 garlic cloves, peeled and chopped
2 beefsteak tomatoes, sliced
a couple of handfuls of fresh marjoram leaves or chopped
    fresh parsley, and extra to serve
½ tin mug of white wine
sea salt and black pepper

Cover the base of a large saucepan or casserole with olive oil, place over a lively heat and colour the aubergine chunks – you can add a drop more oil when turning them. Add the rest of the ingredients with 1/3 of a tin mug of oil and give everything a stir. Once the liquid comes to the boil, cover and cook over a low heat for 1–1¼ hours, or until the potatoes are tender, stirring halfway through. There will be lots of juices, so turn the heat up a tad and continue to cook, uncovered, until the juices concentrate by about a third, another 15 minutes or so. Serve with more herbs scattered over.

Kit Stove or tripod, saucepan or casserole, sharp knife

ANDY WARHOL CHICKEN CASSEROLE

For 3–4 people

Making and taking a spaghetti sauce for your first night away is one route to calming frazzled nerves. It's just not very 'camping', whereas this casserole, which cheats all the way, is at least a stab at something homemade. It is pretty much what you might imagine from the title, and very fine too in a faux 1960s dinner party way. A tin of mushroom soup forms the basis of a sauce for chicken (those 'mini' fillets ensure there is no chopping to be done).

A little in the way of fresh parsley at the end works wonders to whisk it back into the gourmet world. And tomorrow we will wake up feeling totally refreshed, the sun will be shining, and we will cook, properly.

a slug of vegetable or olive oil
a couple of handfuls of lardons (1 x 100g packet)
a couple of handfuls of button mushrooms
500–600g mini chicken fillets
$^1/_3$ tin mug of white wine
1 x 400g can of cream of mushroom soup
sea salt and black pepper
chopped fresh parsley or watercress

Heat a slug of oil in a large saucepan or casserole over a medium heat and fry the lardons with the mushrooms until lightly golden. Stir in the chicken fillets, then add the wine and simmer to reduce it by about half. Add the soup, a little salt and some pepper and simmer the casserole, covered, for 10 minutes, until the chicken is just tender. Stir in a handful or two of chopped parsley or watercress.

To eat
Savoury Rice (see page 151) or buttered spuds.

Kit Stove or tripod, saucepan or casserole, sharp knife

CHICKEN TAGINE WITH PINE NUTS AND RAISINS

For 4–6 people

While a chicken normally only does for 4 people – 5 at a push – the *raison d'être* of a tagine is as much the gravy or juices as the meat, so this will stretch to 6. And it would also be good for guinea fowl, either a nice large one or a couple of small ones.

1 free-range chicken (1.6–1.7 kg), jointed
2 beefsteak tomatoes, cored and sliced
2 onions, peeled and chopped
1 tin mug of red wine
2 teaspoons Moroccan Spice Blend (see page 29)
sea salt and black pepper
a handful of pine nuts
a handful of raisins

Mélange all the ingredients except for the pine nuts and raisins in a large saucepan or casserole. Bring to the boil, cover and cook gently for 1 hour, stirring in the pine nuts and raisins 15 minutes before the end.

To eat
Chopped coriander, couscous or quinoa, or warm flatbreads.

Kit Stove or tripod, saucepan or casserole, sharp knife

POT-ROAST PORK SHOULDER WITH ANCHOVIES AND FENNEL

For 6–8 people

A big-splash roast that serves a decent number of people, and very inexpensively. The meat is exquisitely tender by the end, hardly recognisable as pork at all, more like veal.

At home I would probably sear the joint to colour it before cooking, but this has as much to do with the appearance as anything else. It is sufficiently lavish, with its anchovy and fennel sauce, without doing so.

Fennel is a plant that grows bountifully in the wild and is easily recognised by the most timid of foragers, with its luminous umbrella-shaped flowering heads and familiar feathery fronds. A few of these fronds, along with some of the young fresh seeds scattered over the pork at the end, will give it a little extra allure.

extra virgin olive oil
10 salted anchovy fillets
$^{1}/_{3}$ teaspoon dried chilli flakes
sea salt and black pepper
1 x 1.8–2kg pork shoulder
6 garlic cloves, peeled
1½ tin mugs of white wine
2 fennel bulbs, outer sheath discarded, halved downwards and sliced

Drizzle a few tablespoons of oil over the base of a large saucepan or casserole. Arrange the anchovy fillets in a single layer, scatter over the chilli flakes, then season the pork all over and place fat side down on top. Scatter the garlic cloves around the joint and pour over a mug of wine. Bring to the boil, then reduce the heat, cover and simmer over a low heat for 2½ hours in total, until the meat is meltingly tender. Turn the joint and add the remaining ½ mug of wine after the first hour, and add the fennel about 30 minutes before the end of cooking. Skim the juices of fat before serving.

To eat
Some warm flatbreads and a big green salad are just as good here as a bowl of spuds.

Kit Stove or tripod, saucepan or casserole, sharp knife

COWBOY COFFEE BEEF

For 4–6 people

When our son Louis was very small he bypassed the usual first-word stage and went straight to sentences. Every morning he would sit on our bed and say, 'Corffee? No tank you corffee,' which has always confounded us. Not because he spoke in sentences, but neither of us could think of a single occasion when offered a cup of coffee in bed that we would have said 'no'. Especially when camping, it is the greatest of small luxuries.

Hang on to the rest of the pot for this beef, a curiosity, though by the end there isn't the slightest hint of what lies behind the copious rich beef broth, it just has a delicious cowboyish savour. This is more liquid than I would normally start off with, allowing for cooking over a slightly higher heat than normal – very low flames have a habit of blowing out. The gravy won't go to waste with some buttery spuds, while noodles and macaroni are also fine sops.

about 1kg braising beef, cut into pieces, ideally the size of a plum
1½ tin mugs of coffee
1½ tin mugs of red wine
1 head of garlic, top cut off, papery skin removed
a couple of bay leaves
sea salt
a large pinch of dried chilli flakes or black pepper
4 large carrots, peeled and thickly sliced
a couple of handfuls of shallots, peeled

Place the beef in a large saucepan or casserole with the coffee, wine, garlic, bay leaves, salt and chilli or black pepper. Bring to the boil, skim off any foam and simmer covered for 2 hours, adding the carrots and shallots halfway through. Everything should be meltingly tender by the end. The insides of the garlic can be squeezed out and mashed into the juices.

To eat
Buttered macaroni or spuds.

Kit Stove or tripod, saucepan or casserole, sharp knife

THE GRILL

When we're at home we 'play' barbecues, whereas when we're camping we 'live' barbecues. There is something rather thrilling about being reliant on an open fire to cook with, rather than knowing you can always finish off whatever you're grilling indoors if everything goes wrong. The hardcore camping approach where you start from scratch, building a little fire with wood scattered around, protecting it from the wind with rocks, is hugely satisfying. It's very easy, and opens the way not just for grilling but for one-pot cooking also. This is assuming that you are camping somewhere that it is allowed, and sadly as land becomes more restricted and regulated the opportunities are fewer. So a little travelling barbecue is a good safety net when the countryside won't license such fun.

My portable barbecue is the first item I put out to pack, and it sits there like an expectant dog waiting for a walk, long before such niceties as a tent have been spared a thought. This and a camping stove are the foundation of the traveller's kitchen. I've explored the choices in a little more detail in the chapter Essential Kit (see pages 13–16), but ultimately I urge you to go for a mini-kettle type or covered barbecue. This provides an all-weather solution – if it's chucking it down or blowing a gale, you will still be able to cook up a gorgeous shoulder of lamb or sticky roast chicken. I know this from experience: I have been soaked through, freezing cold and close to tears and dinner has still been fantastic, surreally at odds with the conditions. And suddenly it all seems worth it again.

The second *raison d'être* of a covered grill is being able to roast larger cuts by creating a kind of oven, and that broadens out your options. That said, there is no reason why you can't cook any of the small cuts here on an open barbecue (provided the weather is fine), and ward off any flare-ups with the occasional flick of water.

If I was allowed to take everything on my wish list (this one's always down to negotiation), I would pack a chimney starter too (see page 15). These don't come small, so you might have to do some fairly serious bargaining, but they are foolproof for the fire-shy. You don't even need firelighters – just stuff a couple of pieces of newspaper in the base, light it with your coals in the chimney above and 30 to 40 minutes later they will be blazing away.

I'd like to sneak in that one final tip, something I always forget as it goes against nature – start that little bit earlier than you think you need to. For some reason barbecues always take longer than anticipated, not least because most charcoal advertises allowing about half the time it actually needs to get really hot before you start cooking. If the received wisdom is 20 minutes, then I would give it 45. Wait until the coals are properly coated in a fine dusting of grey ash, moving them around if necessary. If you put the food on and cover the barbecue when they are still only half-coated in ash, there is every chance they will stay that way. And no amount of guitar playing around the fire is going to soothe the wounded pride of the cook. The next pop at harmony will be that rum before bed.

OYSTERS WITH GARLIC BUTTER

Looking at a box of **oysters** sitting beside the tent one day (often one of the great treats when you are camping close to the coast in northern Europe), I thought, 'There has to be an easy way in there.' Then on from that, 'Given that mussels steam open on the grill, as do all manner of clams, why shouldn't oysters?' And they do, in a very hot covered barbecue, behave like any other tenacious bivalve.

Timing is all, however. Three minutes in a covered barbecue over a high heat and just a few will have started to peek open; give it 4 minutes and they should all have done so, retaining that slippery delicacy for which we love them raw. But a minute beyond this and they will turn woolly. So place them cupped side down and cook them just long enough to be able to slip a knife in the crack and lever the shell open.

And while they are grilling (or you are opening them up), melt some **garlic butter** (see page 150) in a small pan. Lift off the flat lid and with it the oyster, pour over any juices in the cupped half and spoon over the melted butter.

Kit Barbecue, saucepan

GOAT'S CHEESE WRAPPED IN PARMA HAM

For about 6 people before supper, or 3 as a light lunch or dinner

You can spin this out with some toasted sourdough, a little green salad, semi-dried tomatoes and the like.

5–6 slices of Parma or other air-dried ham
1 x approx. 15cm medium-mature goat's cheese log

First wrap a slice of ham around each end of the cheese, and then wind the remainder around the length. The idea is to contain the molten cheese so it doesn't drip on to the grill – but don't worry if you find a little works its way out as you're cooking.

Grill on the grid of a hot barbecue until golden all over. The cheese should be molten around the edges, and warm and mousse-like within.

To eat
Oatcakes or other crackers, or warmed pittas.

Kit Barbecue

MUSTARD AND HONEY COCKTAIL SAUSAGES

For 4 people

Strange, given how good cocktail sausages are, how curiously hard to find they can be. But the solution is simple – buy some chipolatas, give each one about 4 twists in the centre, as though making a balloon animal at a children's party, and snip into cocktail sausages.

Thread 500g **cocktail sausages** on to flat metal skewers, piercing them through the middle (as opposed to lengthways) and leaving a little space between them so they can cook evenly. Barbecue them for 5–10 minutes, until half cooked, turning them as necessary and moving them to the outside of the bars if they appear to be colouring too quickly. Brush with 2 tablespoons of **Camping Glaze** (see page 28) and barbecue for another 5–10 minutes until golden and sticky. The glaze will colour very quickly, so keep a careful eye.

Kit Barbecue, skewers

GLAMPING SAUSAGES

This one's good for a crowd, especially all those chic bohemian friends who are expecting more from you than a sausage on a stick.

You want a really meaty sausage here: anything French, in which bread doesn't feature, such as a Toulouse. Grill as many **sausages** as you will need over a barbecue or fire – if you're more than 6 the best route will almost certainly be to create your own barbecue with a large grid over an open fire. I find these normally take about 20 minutes, and there's no need to oil or prick them. At the same time open lots of **oysters** (or grill these too, see page 114), and serve the two together with a big pot of **Crushed Potatoes** (see page 148) and a **green salad** (see page 136).

Kit Barbecue, stove and sharp knife for potatoes

GRILLED PORK CHOPS WITH AIOLI

For 4 people

Pork chops grill up a treat on a barbecue: the ideal is really nice fat juicy ones, which will be divine with a pungent aioli sauce.

4 juicy pork chops
extra virgin olive oil
4 sprigs of fresh rosemary
6 sprigs of fresh thyme
6 tablespoons mayonnaise
4 tablespoons Camping Marinade (see page 27)
sea salt and black pepper

About an hour before grilling, marinate the chops in a bowl or container with a few tablespoons of olive oil and the needles and leaves from the rosemary and thyme. To make the aioli, put the mayonnaise and Camping Marinade into a bowl and blend with a spoon.

Season the chops and grill for a few minutes each side over a very hot barbecue, until golden and firm when pressed. Serve with the aioli.

Kit Barbecue

MIDDLE EASTERN LAMB CHOPS

For 4 people

Delicious with A Kind of Baba Ghanoush (see page 142) and Smoky Courgette Salad (see page 137).

8 juicy lamb cutlets or chops
8 tablespoons Camping Marinade (see page 27)
2 teaspoons Middle Eastern Spice Blend (see page 29)

About an hour before grilling, put the chops into a bowl or container with the Camping Marinade and spice blend and leave to marinate.

Grill the chops for a few minutes each side over a very hot barbecue, until golden but with a slight give to leave them medium rare.

Extra thyme
If you have a few stalks of fresh thyme with you, strip half the leaves off and scatter these and the stalks over when grilling.

Kit Barbecue

GLASTONBURY JERK CHICKEN

For 4 people

The smell of jerk chicken sizzling on a grill is more likely to get me to Glastonbury than any other aspect of the festival. But if you get to have a little dance with dinner, so much the better. Or just grill it up at home and have a little dance in any case.

Chicken fillets or 'mini' chicken fillets are the ideal here, as they cook through with ease, whereas legs and drumsticks take longer and need care to prevent them from drying out before they are fully cooked in the centre.

4 tablespoons Camping Marinade (see page 27)
2 teaspoons Jerk Seasoning (see page 29)
mini chicken fillets to serve 4

Up to a couple of hours before grilling, combine the marinade with the Jerk Seasoning in a bowl or airtight container, then add the chicken and coat it. Cover and set aside if not cooking straight away. Barbecue over hot coals for a few minutes each side – the chicken should feel firm when pressed, and don't worry if it isn't deep gold all over, pale will do. The important thing is to catch it while it's still succulent.

Kit Barbecue

GRILLED SARDINES

For 4 people

Taking in the scent of sardines grilling out of doors is one of the best ways of transporting yourself to some warm Mediterranean shore. It's a fingers-in feast with a juicy tomato salad and some buttered brown bread, or perhaps a couscous salad if the weather suggests it.

Sardines are very delicate little fish – one reason why some fishmongers won't gut them for you (though it's worth asking) – and they also tend to emerge from a barbecue looking a little ragged, which I don't mind, but one of those fish clamps will preserve their silvery form and saves on turning them individually, in which case you may need to allow an extra minute or so. The grill plate of a Cobb also offers a non-stick surface and leaves the sardines intact.

8 good-sized sardines, cleaned and scaled
6 tablespoons Camping Marinade
   (see page 27)
½–1 teaspoon Moroccan Spice Blend
   (see page 29)

You can ask your fishmonger to scale the sardines for you, though they'll probably still need a good wash to completely remove the scales. Pat them dry.

Pour the Camping Marinade over the sardines in a large bowl, scatter over the Moroccan Spice Blend and turn the fish to coat them using your hands. Grill on a barbecue for a few minutes each side, until golden and the fish comes away from the backbone.

Kit Barbecue, fish clamp (optional)

FISH BAKED IN NEWSPAPER

In our camp we're rather fond of this frontier method, which allows us the fantasy that we're camping wild somewhere in the mountains with nothing more than a fishing rod and a good newspaper for company.

This way of cooking small whole fish has the same austerity as steaming them between long wild grasses (see page 126): it keeps the flesh beautifully moist and traps every ounce of the fish's flavour within the paper shell. Like so many radically simple dishes, however, it is not necessarily the easiest to get right. It is often suggested that the parcels are baked in the embers of a fire, but the dividing line between embers and ashes is a fine one. It's not the kind of dish you can test halfway through, as once the parcel is open you have to proceed with eating it, and I reckon the grid of a covered travelling barbecue is a better option. I would serve the fish with Campfire Tagine Tomato Sauce (see page 144), some pittas and also, in a perfect world, some buttered samphire.

Any small fish are candidates, but I have a particular soft spot for **gilthead bream**, which combines everything that is good about plaice and sea bass, rolling them into one – buttery sweetness with a firm succulence. A couple of fish weighing in at 500g each will do for 4 people, though that said, you'll probably polish them off even if there are only 2 of you. Others to try are **trout**, organically farmed **sea bass**, and **grey mullet**. You probably want about 150g per person of filleted fish, so allow double that for a whole unfilleted fish. You may find the fish conveniently weigh in at about 300g each, but if they're more like 500–600g allow one between two people.

Season each fish liberally all over with **sea salt**, including the cavity, and wrap in about 5 sheets of **newspaper**, wetting each sheet first. This gives a more secure parcel than if you simply wet a wodge of paper. Cook the parcels for about 15 minutes a side in a covered barbecue – there is no likelihood of the paper actually bursting into flames, even though you might think there is, but you may need to flick some water at the parcels now and again if the edges of the paper start to smoke. By the end the newspaper will be blackened, but once cut open the skin of the fish should come away with the paper, revealing beautifully cooked milky white flesh.

Kit Barbecue

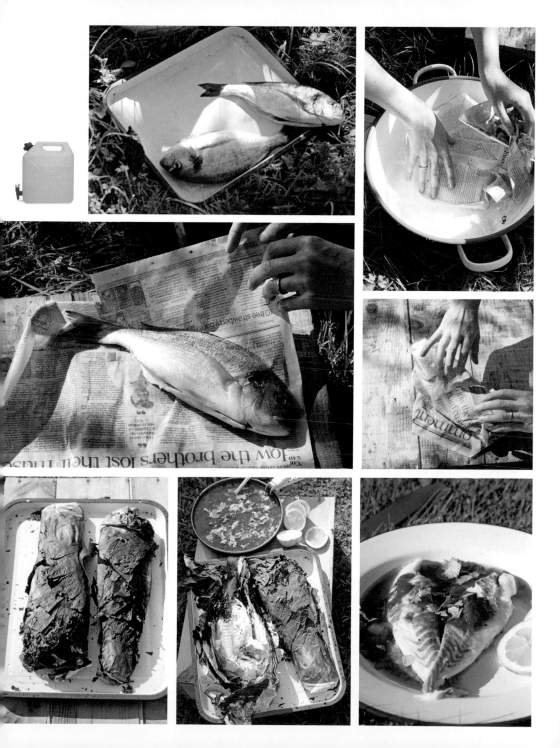

WHOLE FISH STEAMED BETWEEN WILD GRASSES

A lovely way of cooking any whole fish, where long wild grasses scent the flesh as it grills, keeping it moist at the same time. **Salmon, trout, large trout, a small salmon or sea bass** and their ilk are all candidates. A salmon will take around 30 minutes a side, while something smaller should do with about 20 minutes a side. As with Fish Baked in Newspaper (see page 124), allow about 500–600g of whole unfilleted fish for 2 people.

Ask for the fish to be gutted and scaled, and season it well with **sea salt and pepper** inside and out. You can also score the flesh diagonally and stuff the slits with some chopped herbs – **chives, chervil, parsley, tarragon** and the like will all be good – and some finely pared **lemon zest** and seasoning. Keep any adornment as simple as the fish: a **herb mayonnaise**, or **butter** melted with **herbs** and a little **lemon**.

Moisten an armful of **long wild grasses** and spread half of them over a barbecue grid, covering it well. Lay the fish on top and spread the remaining grasses over so that the fish is completely nested in. The grass will hiss as the fish is steamed. Keep the grass moist by flicking it with water when necessary.

Kit Barbecue

ROAST LAMB WITH SWEET AND SOUR TOMATO SAUCE

For 4 people

Half a lamb shoulder is a good compact roast that is bound to fit on to a travelling kettle barbecue. That said, I've also successfully barbecued a whole shoulder in a Cobb barbecue, by colouring it for about 15 minutes skin down, then cooking it the other way up for 1½ hours in total. Pop some flatbreads on to the grill just before eating – the sauce is deliciously soupy, so there's lots of mopping to do. I'd grill some big portobello mushrooms at the same time, as a side veg.

sea salt and black pepper
½ a lamb shoulder
fresh rosemary sprigs
3 tomatoes, preferably on the vine
2 tong-tips (i.e. 2 tablespoons) of tomato chutney
extra virgin olive oil

Season the lamb shoulder all over and lay it on the grid of a kettle barbecue (e.g. a Weber using the indirect method). Scatter over some

rosemary needles and sprigs, rubbing them into the surface of the meat. Close with a lid and barbecue for about 1 hour, turning the joint halfway through – it should be pink in the centre. Leave to rest for 15 minutes, then carve.

About 30 minutes before the lamb is ready, lay the tomatoes beside the lamb. Remove them at the same time as the lamb, leave to cool a little and then skin and pull the flesh off the cores into a bowl. Add the chutney and some salt, and a good slosh of olive oil, and serve with the lamb.

Kit Barbecue

BUTTERFLIED LEG OF LAMB

For 6 people, or 8 as a glorified sandwich

A butterflied leg of lamb is a great cut, like a big juicy fillet – it cooks in no time at all, and it's one of the barbecue treats of the summer. A whole butterflied leg spreads itself out and demands a large kettle barbecue to cook it on, which is not to stop you halving it and cooking it in two goes on a travelling kettle barbecue. It's just as good having cooled down as eaten hot from the grill, and makes great DIY entertaining for a number of people: all you have to do is lay on a selection of breads, a green salad, and some chutney or perhaps the aioli on page 120.

1 leg of lamb, approx. 2.5kg, butterflied
5 tablespoons Camping Marinade (see page 27)
1 heaped tablespoon fresh thyme leaves
sea salt and black pepper

Open out the butterflied leg of lamb, cut it in half, place the two halves in a bowl or dish and using your hands, coat it on both sides with the Camping Marinade and the thyme.

Season the lamb and barbecue half at a time in a covered kettle barbecue (e.g. a Weber using the indirect method), allowing about 20 minutes each side, and placing it skin down first. It's always an inexact art, so use this as a rough guide – if you stick a knife into the thickest part it should still appear pink. Set this half aside while you cook the second half – first adding another few briquettes to each side, and leaving for about 15 minutes for them to heat up. Carve the lamb across the grain, spooning any juices over the meat.

Kit Barbecue

STICKY ROAST CHICKEN

For 4–5 people

A whole roast chicken is ever a holy grail – transported out of doors it is as comforting as a down duvet and a pair of sheepskin slippers, and is somehow a reminder that we haven't left all civilisation at home. This plays on the Cobb barbecue's great strength of cooking a whole bird with surrounding potatoes – something of a feat considering its size, although the maximum size of chicken to go for is 1.5kg. As for the potatoes, which are a cross between roasted and baked, you want smallish waxy ones rather than large bakers, so that they will cook through with ease. The Very Chunky Mushroom Sauce on page 145 would be my answer to gravy, or at least a sauce, and it doubles up as a veggie too. Anything else? Well, the Sweet Little Peas on page 139 are next on the wish list.

If, however, you don't have a Cobb, a travelling Weber using the indirect method (see page 14) is another solution. Halve the chicken as though spatchcocking it, cutting first through the base and then the breastbone, which you can cut out if you wish. Drizzle over a little oil, season, then coat the chicken skin with the glaze and barbecue it, covered, for 45 minutes, skin down for half the time and then turning it the right way up. This is also a lovely way of cooking a guinea fowl. These tend to come up smaller – a good-sized one of 1.2–1.3kg will do for 4 people max.

vegetable or olive oil
1 x 1.5kg free-range chicken (untrussed)
sea salt and black pepper
2 tablespoons Camping Glaze (see page 28)
8 medium waxy potatoes, scrubbed

Fuel your Cobb with a cobblestone (see page 35) – if using charcoal briquettes, the cooking time will be longer.

Drizzle a little oil over your chicken and season it. Grill it either on a roasting rack or on the grill plate of a Cobb for 1½ hours – giving it 10 minutes on each breast initially to colour it before turning it the right way up. Drizzle over the Camping Glaze halfway through.

At the same time as putting the chicken on, rub some oil over the potatoes, season with salt and cook them around the bird, turning them halfway through when you glaze the chicken. You can leave these on the grill while you rest the chicken for 15–20 minutes, rearranging them so that they colour evenly.

Kit Barbecue

SIDE ORDERS

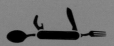

A passion for vegetables doesn't diminish just because we are camping, it simply gets that little bit harder to deliver all those lovely asides that we take for granted when we're at home. But fear not, because nothing that follows is even vaguely challenging.

Starting with the no-cook route, a green salad and a pile of warm pittas are the quickest way of rounding off any number of offerings, and often the most welcome. And here the Camping Marinade (see page 27) and Camping Glaze (see page 28) come up trumps – combine the two and you have a sophisticated little salad dressing with the hints of garlic, mustard and honey that are so central to a good vinaigrette. Take along a couple of spare lockable plastic containers and you can make up plenty without risk of it leaking while you are on the move.

Next, with the kind of relaxed fare we're after, we need to involve the grill. A barbecue offers up all sorts of Med-inspired deliciousness, starting with Provençal vegetables,

the trio of aubergines, courgettes and tomatoes, all of which can be chucked on to the grill whole, and are readily souped up once cooked into mezze-type dishes with the help of the Camping Marinade and a few spices. While on the one-pot front the Smothered French Beans (see page 141) is a huge favourite, and in fact I could happily eat these with every meal – a little stew where tomatoes, onions and garlic fuse into a rich oily sauce that coats whatever green or yellow beans you have to hand as they gently cook.

On to carbs. We need these when we're camping. Being pleasantly satiated is no longer enough, we need to feel 'full', with a few calories to spare, laid down for emergencies. Frequently the greatest no-no is a strainer – you might have one with you but quite likely you might not, and you are spared the need in most of what follows. The very simplest is couscous: simply add boiling water, a slug of olive oil and some salt and ten minutes later it's at the ready for eating hot with soupy stews or at a later date cold in a salad. This way of cooking rice, in which it cooks by the 'absorption method', doesn't sound very alluring but in practice leaves you with perfectly fluffy grains and a clean pan, while Crushed Potatoes are the answer to 'mashed', and suitably rustic. Or why not make some garlic bread, a goer with pretty much everything, but especially My Big Fat Chilli con Carne (see page 98) and No-chop Spaghetti Puttanesca (see page 93) that share the same retro hat.

There are also a couple of ideas for sauces, if not as we know them. Barbecued offerings relish something gloopy to mop up with all that buttery garlic bread and those pittas. In Campfire Tagine Tomato Sauce big tomatoes are filled with a little spice, garlic and olive oil and cooked on the barbecue until soft. Scoop out the insides and you have a ready-made sauce. Or grill mushrooms filled with crème fraîche, then coarsely chop them, and

the juices combine with the cream to create a lovely chunky sauce that's especially good with chicken and grilled fish. As ever, don't wait to go camping to exploit the ease of these – a barbecue in the back garden is just as good an opportunity.

SOMETHING GREEN

THE SIMPLE SOLUTION

The easiest route to rounding off any grill or one-pot dish is to serve a big green salad and lots of bread, neither of which will hog the grill or that one precious ring.

BREAD

If your bread is fresh there's no further ado, but the greatest convenience when camping is pittas and other flatbreads that can be warmed on the grill for a minute or two after you have taken whatever you are cooking off it, or in a frying pan on a gas ring for an equally short time. They keep for days, and it goes without saying that they can't get squashed.

A GREEN SALAD

Lovely as big blowsy **lettuces** are, they take a lot of washing, and tightly closed hearts or heads are a better option. **Little Gems**, **Romaine lettuce hearts** and **chicory** are personal favourites. This is the time as well to turn to bags of pre-washed leaves – I tend to favour single leaves over the mixes, so **watercress**, **rocket** and **lamb's lettuce** are all good. You can mix these in with other leaves from hearts or with a few **sprouting seeds** and the like.

Kit Sharp knife

A TOMATO SALAD

Tomato salads don't have to try very hard to be chic, especially during the summer months. A serrated knife will make light work of any selection of **tomatoes** you have acquired. Season them with **salt** and pour over a slug of **extra virgin olive oil**, and scatter with a little chopped **fresh parsley** or a few slivers of **spring onion**, should you have them.

Kit Sharp knife

SMOKY COURGETTE SALAD

For 4 people

At home I painstakingly thinly slice and then grill my courgettes, whereas here, to make life easier, they are grilled first and then cut up and dressed. You can spin this dish out with some fresh goat's cheese and black olives.

Drizzle some **extra virgin olive oil** over 6 small **courgettes** and season with **salt and pepper**. Barbecue for 20–40 minutes, until nicely coloured and softened. Leave to cool a little, then cut off the ends, pop them into a bowl and coarsely chop. Add a few tablespoons of olive oil, a squeeze of **lemon juice**, some salt and pepper, and a handful of **pine nuts** and **fresh Greek basil leaves** or torn **fresh mint leaves**. Eat slightly warm or at room temperature.

Kit Barbecue, sharp knife

HONEY-MUSTARD SALAD DRESSING

Enough for a good couple of salads for 3–4 people

Place 2 teaspoons of **Camping Glaze** (see page 28) in a small airtight container or jar with 6 tablespoons of **Camping Marinade** (see page 27), put the lid on and give it a good shake.

CUCUMBER AND FETA COUSCOUS

For 4 people

If you weren't very keen on couscous before you started camping, you are about to start loving it. With no cooking involved, it is perfect for the occasion, makes great salads and is lovely with soupy tagines and stews.

1 tin mug of couscous
extra virgin olive oil
sea salt
½ a cucumber, quartered and thinly sliced
a few small fresh mint leaves, torn
6 tablespoons Camping Marinade (see page 27)
a couple of handfuls of pitted green olives
1 x 200g block of feta cheese, coarsely crumbled

Combine the couscous, a slug of olive oil and a pinch of salt in a large bowl, then pour over 1½ tin mugs of boiling water and set aside. It will be ready in 10 minutes, but for the purposes of this salad, leave it to cool and then fluff it up. Mix in all the remaining salad ingredients, adding the feta last. Splash over a little more oil before eating.

Kit Sharp knife

SWEET LITTLE PEAS

For 4 people

If frozen petit pois are a British staple, then in France it is tinned petit pois, or further up the scale petit pois in jars. Either way the Gallic preference is more convenient than frozen when camping.

Place a 400g **tin drained petit pois**, a couple of knobs of **butter**, a **sliced lettuce heart**, a sprig of **mint** if you have one, and a little **salt** in a medium-sized pan, cover and cook over a low heat for 10 minutes.

Kit Stove, saucepan, sharp knife

GRILLED CORN WITH SAGE AND LEMON

For 4 people

Drizzle some **extra virgin olive oil** over 4 **corn cobs**, stripped of their outer husk and silk, and trimmed top and bottom, and season them with **salt and pepper**. Barbecue for about 20 minutes, until nicely golden all over, then remove them to a plate while you make the butter.

Pop a large frying pan on to the barbecue and melt about a third of a 250g packet of **unsalted butter**. Once the foam starts to calm, scatter a handful of **sage leaves** and the pared **zest of a lemon** (though this is optional) over the surface and fry until the leaves darken and crisp, then remove from the heat and stir in 5 tablespoons of extra virgin olive oil. Serve this spooned over the corn, with a squeeze of **lemon juice**, scattered with sea salt. The sage leaves will be good to eat, while the lemon zest is there purely to scent.

Kit Barbecue, frying pan, sharp knife

FONDUE LEEKS

For 4 people as a side, or 2 people as a main

Like all good fondues you need to stand attendant on these and set to eating them the minute they come off the grill. Spin them out with some honey-roast ham, and you have a feast of a supper.

Drizzle some **extra virgin olive oil** over 8 good-sized **leeks** (or 4 if they are real prize winners), trimmed top and bottom, and season with **salt and pepper**. Don't worry about removing the tough outer layers – these serve as a cooking shell and will be discarded. Grill on a covered barbecue for 20–30 minutes, turning them halfway through, until they are blackened on the outside and a knife inserts with ease.

Slit the leeks open and arrange cut side up on one or two pieces of foil, cupping the edges. Drizzle over a little oil, season and cover with thin slices of **Gruyère**, **Beaufort** or **Comte**. Drizzle over a little more oil, scatter over some **fresh thyme leaves,** slip the foil back on to the grill and cook covered for another 10 minutes, until the cheese has melted. Eat just the insides of the leeks with the melted cheese, discarding the charred exterior.

Kit Barbecue, sharp knife, foil

SMOTHERED FRENCH BEANS

For 4 people

The summer brings with it French beans of every variety – grown close to home in the summer months, we can choose from yellow or green, skinny or fat. They travel well, don't require any chilling and call for minimum preparation. It's a pleasurable, idle 10 minutes spent sitting in the late afternoon sun nicking off the tops with your fingers.

1 large handful of green or yellow beans per person, tops trimmed, halved if long
2 tomatoes, sliced
2 garlic cloves, peeled and sliced
sea salt and black pepper
1 onion, peeled, halved and sliced
3 tablespoons extra virgin olive oil, plus extra for drizzling
a handful of chopped fresh parsley, chervil or chives (optional)

Bung everything except for the herbs into a medium saucepan, pop the lid on and cook over a gentle heat for 30–40 minutes, checking on them occasionally, until the beans are tender and sitting in a light tomato sauce. Serve with a drizzle of oil, scattered with some parsley, chervil or chives if you have any to hand.

Kit Stove, saucepan, sharp knife

A KIND OF BABA GHANOUSH

For 4 people

Aubergines and tomatoes are two of the most successful vegetables to grill on a barbecue – they don't even require oil or seasoning – simply throw them on whole. The aubergines will take about 45 minutes to cook, so you will probably need to put these on before any meat that is part of the feast. This is delicious served with barbecued merguez or other spicy sausages, and warm flatbread.

4 aubergines
3 tomatoes, preferably on the vine
3 tablespoons Camping Marinade (see page 27)
1 teaspoon Middle Eastern Spice Blend (optional) (see page 29)
sea salt
extra virgin olive oil
a handful of coarsely chopped fresh flat-leaf parsley

Prick the aubergines all over to stop them bursting, and grill on a barbecue for about 45 minutes until the skin is blackened and blistered, turning them now and again. Grill the tomatoes on the vine for about 20 minutes, turning them once. Leave both to cool a little, then skin the aubergines and coarsely chop the flesh in a bowl using a knife and fork. If there is any excess liquid pour it off, pressing it out using a fork. Skin the tomatoes and add the flesh to the bowl, crushing it with your fingers. Mix in the Camping Marinade, the spice blend and some salt, then splash over some oil and scatter over the parsley.

Kit Barbecue, sharp knife

A COUPLE OF SAUCES

CAMPFIRE TAGINE TOMATO SAUCE

For 4 people

A deliciously smoky sauce for ladling over any grilled meat or fish, which is baked within the tomato shell. It can also be made in advance and gently reheated, adding the coriander at the last minute.

3 good-sized beefsteak tomatoes
sea salt
1 teaspoon Moroccan Spice Blend (see page 29)
1 garlic clove, peeled and crushed to a paste
extra virgin olive oil
a handful of coarsely chopped fresh coriander (optional)

Slice the top off each tomato and scoop out the core in the centre, about 2 tablespoons of the flesh in total. Season the cut surface with salt, scatter the spice and garlic in the cavities, and refill with olive oil, almost to the top. Replace the lid, place the tomatoes in a shallow pan such as a Trangia frying pan, and cook in a covered barbecue for 30–45 minutes until softened – you may find there is a pool of juices and some oil in the pan. You can also cook these over an open grid.

Scoop the softened flesh away from the shells, discarding the skin, and stir in the coriander if you have some.

Kit Barbecue, sharp knife, frying pan

A VERY CHUNKY MUSHROOM SAUCE

For 4 people

This is one of those sauces hearty enough to stand in as a vegetable, great for roast chicken in lieu of gravy or with grilled steaks and the like. It neatly occupies the twenty minutes during which the meat is resting, and is especially appealing for late summer camping.

Drizzle some **extra virgin olive oil** over 4 **flat-cap mushrooms**, stalks discarded, and season them with **salt and black pepper**. Grill them in

a covered barbecue cupped-side down for 10 minutes, then turn them, fill the cavities with **crème fraîche** and grill for another 10 minutes. Coarsely chop them in a bowl and add a handful of coarsely chopped **fresh flat-leaf parsley**.

Kit Barbecue, sharp knife

A CARB ON THE SIDE

STOVED ROASTIES

For 4 people

The two types of potato that will most challenge campers (and that's a near guarantee that you'll end up craving them) are roast and baked. These delicious stovies, which are cooked skin on, cut a fine dividing line between the two. The rosemary and garlic make for especially tasty spuds, but without them this is still a good means to an end – there is, however, a pan to wash afterwards. Apologies for that.

a handful of small waxy potatoes per person, scrubbed
extra virgin olive oil
sea salt and black pepper
4 garlic cloves, peeled and halved
a few sprigs of fresh rosemary

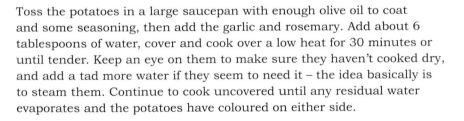

Toss the potatoes in a large saucepan with enough olive oil to coat and some seasoning, then add the garlic and rosemary. Add about 6 tablespoons of water, cover and cook over a low heat for 30 minutes or until tender. Keep an eye on them to make sure they haven't cooked dry, and add a tad more water if they seem to need it – the idea basically is to steam them. Continue to cook uncovered until any residual water evaporates and the potatoes have coloured on either side.

Kit Stove or tripod, saucepan or casserole, sharp knife

BABY BAKED POTATOES

For 4 people

Another take on roast-come-baked potatoes, this time cooked in a parcel on a barbecue – they absorb the wine and scent of the bay leaves and are lovely and oily on the outside. But if you are simply after the most basic way of baking a potato, don't worry about the bay leaves, and water will stand in for wine.

a handful of baby potatoes per person
4 tablespoons extra virgin olive oil
4 tablespoons white wine
sea salt and black pepper
4 bay leaves

Divide the potatoes between two pieces of foil so they sit in a single layer. Drizzle over the oil and wine, season and tuck in the bay leaves. Wrap up into a parcel, then place on a second piece of foil, seam downwards, and wrap up again. Cook in a covered barbecue for 1¼–1½ hours, turning the parcels halfway through.

Kit Barbecue, foil

CRUSHED POTATOES

For 4 people

These potatoes are good barbecue fare for when you want something in between boiled potatoes and a potato salad. They're delicious eaten hot or warm, and I also enjoy them cold.

waxy potatoes for 4 people, peeled or scrubbed as necessary
about 8 tablespoons extra virgin olive oil
a handful of chopped fresh parsley
sea salt

Cook the potatoes in boiling salted water until tender. Drain them in a colander and leave for a few minutes for the surface moisture to evaporate. Return the potatoes to the pan and, using a fork or the back of a spoon, gently crush them into pieces. Pour over the olive oil, scatter over the parsley and season with salt.

Kit Stove, saucepan

GARLIC BREAD

For 1 small baguette

Garlic butter is a good one to make up before you leave home and take with you in an airtight container. As well as being used for garlic bread, melted it makes a fab sauce for all sorts of shellfish – grilled oysters and prawns, razor-shell clams, mussels – or simply grilled fish or chicken.

Blend about a quarter of a 250g packet of **softened unsalted butter** with 2–3 crushed **garlic cloves** and some **salt and black pepper** – in an ideal world I would also add some chopped soft fresh herbs such as **parsley** or **chives**.

Either thickly slice the **baguette**, leaving the pieces attached at the base, and generously spread the butter on either side of each slice, or slit it in half horizontally and spread the butter top and bottom. Depending on the size of your barbecue, you may need to halve it first. Wrap it up in foil. Heat it on the grid of a barbecue or in a frying pan on a stove for about 5 minutes each side.

Kit Barbecue, or stove and frying pan, foil, sharp knife

SAVOURY RICE

For 4 people

A great method for cooking rice if you don't have a colander to call on. By a simple absorption process, you should be left with a pretty clean pan at the end. You can spice this up with chicken or vegetable stock (cubes are fine), and serve the rice plain or add whatever takes your fancy – some slivers of roasted vegetables, crispy bacon, toasted nuts, or chopped herbs and olive oil. It can be eaten hot, or used for salads once it's cool.

1¾ tin mugs of water or chicken or vegetable stock
1 tin mug of basmati rice
1 teaspoon sea salt

If using stock, make this up in a medium saucepan, then add the rice and salt (bearing in mind that you may not need as much liquid if you have used a stock cube). Bring the liquid to the boil and simmer for 8–10 minutes, then cover the pan, remove from the heat and leave to stand for 20 minutes. Fluff the rice up with a fork to serve.

Kit Stove, saucepan

SWEET CHIC

It is easy to see why marshmallows (and bananas) are the camping hit that they are, as they capture the moment after supper so perfectly, when you want something sweet to go out on, but ideally without having to lift a finger – not least because it is getting dark and you can't see what you're doing. If you're not careful you risk waking up to colonies of ants marching purposefully through your tent. So this chapter is really an extension of that way of thinking, which shamelessly expoits any sweet (and fruit) that is up for being grilled, not just marshmallows but those bons-bons and the like, nougat and even jelly babies.

One of the best ways of showing your age is to recall how the village newsagent used to sell sweets by the weight from large jars lining the walls, served by a lady behind a counter who tipped them into a brown paper bag. But frankly you don't have to be that old. It's simply that these days it seems you have to go to Harrods or Fortnum & Mason for them, or online to some recherché website. Otherwise you are most likely to find such delights in some hidden-away corner shop in the middle of nowhere, forgotten by time.

Which makes them all the more practical, with little pots of fromage blanc (those petits suisses that are so good dusted with caster sugar are just right). Try them with grilled bons-bons – sugar-dusted sweets with toffee inside that when warmed over the fire make a great brûlée topping. And the old grilled bananas are ever a winner, blackened over the barbecue, then slit and filled with the chocolate of your choice; while pretty much any fruit, and in particular stone fruits and figs, will be divine dipped into water and then into sugar and grilled until they caramelise.

If you insist that it has to be a real, full-on pudding, I would suggest wrapping a hunk of cake (such as the chocolate or ginger cakes on pages 59 and 65) in foil and warming it for about 5 minutes either side on the barbecue or in a frying pan – *et voilà*, a sponge pud that you can drizzle with syrup or eat with a squirt of cream.

JELLY BABY KEBABS

Something of a Joan of Arc moment here, but thread 4 **jelly babies**, of different flavours, through the waist on to a metal or soaked wooden skewer. Gently heat them close to the embers of a fire – a barbecue in its dying hour will do fine. You need to catch them just at the right moment, while they still have the composure of their shape, but are liquid gel within, the consistency of one of those beautiful glacé fruits, a whole clementine for instance, that drips with a viscous syrup once you're past its candied shell.

Kit Barbecue, skewers

STRAWBERRY SAUCERS

I could never in a million years have dreamt up a pudding involving flying saucers – it took a child's mind, his brief being that he had to get something healthy in there, if he wanted any sweets at all.

Invest in a large jar of chalky pastel-coloured **flying saucers** – orange and lemon yellow, dusky pink and eau-de-nil. Tap each one to shake the sherbet to the bottom of the shell, then cut off the top and slip in a sliver of **strawberry**.

Kit Sharp knife

STICKY FIGS

Figs are especially good grilled in this fashion. Anything cooked on a barbecue will acquire a slightly smoky scent, but it's not unpleasing, especially if you marry it with a young goat's cheese.

Halve and dip a couple of **figs** per person first into water (or lemon juice) and then into **caster sugar**. Grill either side, cut-side down first, until sticky and golden, and serve with a dollop of **young goat's cheese**.

You could also serve the figs with warm ginger cake instead of the cheese – lovely if there's any left over from the Famous Five's picnic (see page 65), but otherwise McVitie's Jamaica Ginger Cake. To warm the cake, wrap it in foil and sit it on the grid of a barbecue for about 5 minutes either side.

Kit Barbecue

BON-BON BRÛLÉES

For this you want the old-fashioned **sugared bons-bons** with toffee within. Allow a couple per person, popped on to the end of skewers. Grill over a barbecue or in a fire until the sugar on the outside has caramelised, meaning that the toffee within will have melted to a lovely goo. Slip this on top of a **petit suisse**, for a faux crème brûlée.

Kit Barbecue or fire, skewers

APRICOTS WITH GOOEY NOUGAT

For 2 people

Cooked apricots turn divinely tender, sweet and sour. How can anyone not like them? Yet I live in a household where they are shunned, even by my children's friends. But I'm not giving up, because there's a small chance that you just might love them as much as I do.

4 apricots, halved and stoned
a knob of butter
1 tablespoon dark rum
2 pieces of nougat

Arrange the apricot halves on a piece of foil and make the sides of the foil into a boat. Dot the fruit with the butter, drizzle over the rum, then place a sliver of nougat in each apricot half. Cook in a covered barbecue for 10–15 minutes, until the fruit and nougat are softened.

Kit Barbecue, foil, sharp knife

PIRATE BANANAS

For 4 people

A classic, and understandably so.

Grill 4 **bananas**, skin on, on a barbecue for about 5 minutes each side until blackened and softened. Transfer them to a large plate or a board, slit them open down the middle and pop a few squares of **milk or dark chocolate** into the centre of each one. Set aside for a few minutes for this to melt, then gently open up the bananas.

The Adult Version
A little **dark rum or whisky** drizzled over, which you can warm and ignite first if inclined.

The Child Version
A squirt of **shaving-foam cream** (great stuff when camping) down the centre, or a dollop of sticky **unpasteurised or clotted cream**.

Inbetweenies
A bit of **rum**, a bit of **cream**.

Kit Barbecue, sharp knife

CRÊPES SUZETTE

For 4 people

Dedicated to my late father-in-law, Tony Bell, a great showman who never as far as I know cooked a meal in his life, like so many men of his generation. But he would take centre stage at dinner parties, my poor mother-in-law having toiled all afternoon making lacy fine pancakes that he would then finish with a flourish on a portable gas ring with copious amounts of flaming brandy.

Simmer 1 tin mug of **fresh orange juice** (blood orange if you can find it), 1 tablespoon of **caster sugar** and a couple of knobs of **unsalted butter** in

a frying pan until reduced by about half. Add 4 **pancakes** (or 3 if they are especially large), folded in quarters, to the pan one by one and coat them in the syrup. Once they are warmed through, you can flambé them with **dark rum or brandy** for the full-on treat. Warm it over a flame in a tablespoon or small ladle, ignite and carefully pour it over.

Kit Stove, frying pan

GRILLED CHOCOLATE MARSHMALLOWS

Toasted teacakes with a difference, a ready-made s'more, the classic campfire treat of a toasted marshmallow popped between a couple of Graham crackers with a layer of chocolate, partially melting it. **Tunnocks teacakes** provide us with the perfect solution, a marshmallow covered in chocolate with a biscuit below. Skewer these and grill briefly, held over a barbecue or in a fire, until the chocolate appears covered with beads of moisture, by which time the marshmallow will be deliciously mousse-like within.

Kit Barbecue or fire, skewers

S'MORES

These are a kind of make-your-own Tunnocks teacake – skewer and grill **marshmallows**, slip them on to a small thin biscuit such as **chocolate chip shortcake**, and sandwich with a second biscuit. If they are **plain biscuits**, pop a couple of squares of **chocolate** in between along with the marshmallow.

Kit Barbecue or fire, skewers

PEACH CRUMBLE

For 6 people

A cheat of a topping, but no less for that, an instant crumble. You could also scatter over a few pieces of fudge, thinly sliced, to add to the treat. There's no need to lug a special pudding dish along with you – improvise with something to hand. I find the Trangia frying pan does a great job of doubling up as a gratin dish.

3–4 ripe peaches (ideally white), sliced off the stone
2 tablespoons runny honey
4 flapjacks (see page 69), crumbled

Scatter the peach slices over the base of a shallow pan that will hold the peaches in a crowded single layer. Drizzle over the honey, cover with foil and bake on the grid of a covered barbecue for about 10 minutes, until the fruit has softened and is sitting in lots of juices. Scatter over the crumbled flapjack and cook for another 5–10 minutes, again in a covered barbecue but without the foil. Good hot or cold.

Kit Barbecue, frying pan, foil

SUMMER PUD FOR CAMPERS

For 4 people

This deconstructed summer pud will take on board any selection of berries. So it's great for all those blackberries you've risked hands and knees to gather. As ever, divine with clotted and sticky untreated creams, a farmhouse treat should you be camping in a field in dairy country.

2 tin mugs of mixed berries (raspberries, loganberries,
    red and blackcurrants, blackberries, etc.)
3 tablespoons caster sugar
4 small slices of day-old white bread

Gently heat the berries with the sugar in a small covered saucepan for about 10 minutes until they are sitting in lots of juices, stirring halfway through. Leave these to cool. Lay a slice of bread on each of 4 plates, ladle over the fruit and juices and leave to soak in for 10 minutes.

Kit Stove, saucepan

AND SO TO BED

Perhaps the best investment in forward thinking while you have the stove lit is to whiz up a thermos of hot chocolate. It's a hot water bottle in sweet nectar form, just a small cup, with a couple of teaspoons of dark rum in yours, biscuits all round and snuggle down.

The easy route is one of those top-end hot chocolates, where all you need do is pour hot milk over the powder. But there is nothing quite as delicious as properly made cocoa, sipped hands wrapped around mug, sitting at the entrance of your tent as the light is finally fading. Although I suspect there is an entire generation coming on who have no idea how to make it, given how convenience wins over. If you are prepared to wash up the pan it wins hands down.

MUG OF COCOA

For 1 person

The important thing with making cocoa is to cook it, otherwise it will taste powdery and raw. It also needs to be added to warm or hot liquid in order to blend. Place 1 heaped teaspoon of **cocoa** and 1½ teaspoons of **sugar** in a small saucepan, and add a few tablespoons of **milk**. Gently heat until the milk is warm, then blend in the cocoa using the back of a spoon. Add ½ a tin mug of milk and bring to a rolling boil.

Kit Stove, saucepan

REAL CHOCOLATE HOT CHOCOLATE

For 1 person

Another route that saves on having to take a tub of chocolate powder with you is to pour ½ a tin mug of **boiling milk** over a row of **dark chocolate squares** in a mug or bowl – breaking this into small pieces first. Leave it for a few minutes, then stir vigorously to melt. Sweeten to taste, and you could scatter over a few **mini marshmallows** if you feel you haven't had your fill around the campfire.

AND YOURS? I was going to suggest a couple of teaspoons of **rum** splashed in, but depending on the circumstances that may seem a little conservative and something closer to neat spirit might be in order. **Whisky** is another good camping companion – in the interests of an uninterrupted night's sleep you can consider it medicinal.

Kit Stove, saucepan

BEST BISCUITS FOR DUNKING

Chocolate Digestives
Bourbons
Custard Creams
Hobnobs
Scottish Shortbread Fingers

All of which go very well with rum and whisky too.

STOCKISTS

The following websites come recommended for keen campers:

www.seasonedpioneers.co.uk
'Annie's Camping Kit' contains all the spice blends mentioned in the book, that come in convenient resealable foil pouches, or you can order them individually.

www.weber.com
Maker of iconic kettle barbecues. The 'Smokey Joe Gold' is the travel size, or their 'Go-Anywhere' shaped like a box, works on the same principles. You can also obtain chimney starters, odourless firelighters and especially long tongs.

www.cobb-bbq.co.uk
These now familiar domed portable barbecues offer an eco-friendly solution to cooking whole chickens, as well as smaller cuts. They come with a convenient travel case. Cobblestones and accessories can be obtained from the website.

www.millets.co.uk
My favourite dedicated one-stop camping shop, not least for the range of fashionable tents and accessories, designed by luminaries like Celia Birtwell and Zandra Rhodes. It turns teepees into collectors items. They can also be trusted for their range of gas stoves.

www.lakeland.co.uk
This company has a track record for well-tested, user-friendly cooking equipment. They stock excellent flectalon-lined cold-bags, as well as all manner of other equipment recommended in the book such as Lock & Lock storage containers.

www.outdoor-kitchen.biz
This small company specialises in Serbian enamelware, and has an unusual range of products including an enamel water jug and a 'kotlich', a large cooking pot for using with a tripod.

www.johnlewis.co.uk
For sets of stackable Lock and Lock containers. A seven piece should provide plenty of storage options for most camping trips.

www.jwpltd.co.uk
For stockists of Lock & Lock containers.

www.josephjoseph.com
This innovative kitcheware company have big, brightly coloured lightweight solutions that are great for camping. Their magnetic measuring spoon has both teaspoon and tablespoon measures, so all you need in addition is a tin mug. Their stackable bowls come with a colander, a sieve and a lemon squeeze, and double as serving and cooking bowls. Their folding wooden bread board is another great design.

www.greentulip.co.uk
This eco-friendly on-line store offer a large range of lightweight bamboo and cork products.

www.naturallythinking.com
Look sideways to the beauty industry for travel-size aluminium pots and screwtop bottles, for decanting small quantities of foodstuffs.

www.nisbets.co.uk
This on-line supplier of professional equipment is brilliant for inexpensive, hardwearing kit. They stock the one and only 'REX' potato peeler, and travelling knife holders are especially useful.

www.rosle.com
The now old-fashioned vegetable choppers with a blade that you push up and down have been all but replaced by food processors at home, but they still have a place in our 'batterie de cuisine' on field trips.

www.eddingtons.co.uk
The American cast iron foundry Lodge produce classic cookware. Here you will find Dutch ovens in various sizes, tripods and pot lifters, for cooking one-pot dishes in true cowboy style over an open fire.

www.dream-pot.co.uk
This portable slow cooker contains two saucepans. Cook casseroles or one-pot dishes for about a quarter of their normal time, pop them into the insulated 'Dream-Pot' and a couple of hours later you have a piping hot dish at the ready.

www.aolcookshop.co.uk
GreenPan lead the way in eco-friendly cookery technology. Their thermalon coated frying pans are as light as non-stick aluminium and cook like a dream.

www.surplusandoutdoors.com
Enamelware mugs, plates and bowls are core camping kit. They get better and better with wear and tear, stack and pack to nothing, and are unbreakable.

www.chomette.co.uk
If like me you cannot live without a proper peppermill, even when camping, then look no further than Peugeot's miniature 'Bistro' mill.

www.cathkidston.co.uk
Cath's aprons and tea towels are guaranteed to provide a home-making touch in any camping situation, and make the gloomiest of days seem ever sunny.

www.belltent.co.uk
This company specialises in traditional canvas bell-tents, that lend themselves to glamorous bohemian living, and are roomy enough to stand up in and spread out with serious bedding.

www.tartanrugs.com
Regardless of whether you plan on picnicing, a plastic backed rug is bound to come in handy, whether it's to ward off the dew at breakfastime, or to sit on the ground after a shower of rain. They fold away to nothing with convenient carry handles.

www.amazon.co.uk
Thermos Work Series steel flasks are a classic piece of design, that are guaranteed to keep fluids hot or cold for 24 hours. All manner of other camping equipment can also be sourced from this site.

ACKNOWLEDGEMENTS

Writing this book was spontaneous and last-minute, and led to a summer of fun lived out of doors, that wouldn't have been possible without many other people who entered into the spirit and made it all happen.

So with many thanks to:

Kyle Cathie and Judith Hannam, Senior Commissioning Editor, for giving us the opportunity. Lizzy Kremer, my agent at David Higham Associates, whose enthusiasm for camping fuelled the seed of an idea in the first place. Vicky Orchard, Editor, for her endless calm and efficiency. Annie Lee for her eagle eye in copy editing. Georgia Vaux for her splendid design of the book. Salima Hirani, for proofreading the manuscript. Isobel McLean, for her index. Julia Barder, as Sales and Marketing Director. Victoria Scales, for publicity. Jonnie Bell, for picking up a camera after so many years, and snapping away all summer. Louis Bell, our son, Benjamin Goodstein, and Will and Minna Moon White, campers supreme, also Gabi Tubbs. The Beards – Alex, Kate, Betty and Alfie, who thought they were coming to stay for a break. The Boxers – Kate and Charlie, who thought we were coming to stay for a break.

INDEX